Keith Markham qualified as a Solicitor in 2001 and now works as a freelancer providing training and consultancy services.

He began his career in private practice, and then moved in-house at the BGL Group, a major insurance intermediary that includes comparethemarket.com among its brands. During his time there, Keith regularly conducted contract negotiations of a complex nature, often with major blue-chip companies.

Subsequently, Keith joined BPP Professional Education, one of Europe's leading providers of professional development training. He worked there as both an in-house lawyer dealing with commercial contracts and data protection and also as a presenter of training courses before establishing his own consultancy in 2009.

Drawing on his considerable experience, Keith has designed and delivered a wide variety of training for BPP, MBL and other providers as well as for his own clients in the commercial law field. In particular, he teaches topics relating to commercial contracts and data protection to lawyers and non-lawyers alike. He also provides consultancy services to an increasing number of clients in these fields.

He is also the author of '*A Practical Guide to the General Data Protection Regulation*' which is now available in its second edition.

Covid-19, Force Majeure and Frustration of Contracts – The Essential Guide

Covid-19, Force Majeure and Frustration of Contracts – The Essential Guide

Keith Markham
LLB Hons
Solicitor (non-practising)
Freelance Consultant

Law Brief Publishing

Published 2020 by Law Brief Publishing, an imprint of Law Brief Publishing Ltd
30 The Parks
Minehead
Somerset
TA24 8BT

www.lawbriefpublishing.com

Paperback: 978-1-913715-05-2

To the staff and students (past and present) of the Nicolaus Copernicus Peterborough Polish School. My thanks, for allowing an Englishman into your midst, for teaching me the complexities of your language, culture and history and for ensuring that my life as a trustee is never dull, not for a moment.

PREFACE

At the beginning of 2020, the vast majority of contract lawyers could not have foreseen the need, within a short space of time, to dust off their force majeure clauses and remind themselves of the rules on frustration. Nevertheless, the Covid 19 outbreak, and subsequent decisions taken by governments across the world, are likely to provide a fruitful source for disputes for many years to come. The aim of this book is to meet the obvious need for a simple summary of the key rules combined with practical drafting tips. There is a specific focus on the impact of Covid 19 but many of the points made apply more broadly to other events.

The law is as stated on 12th June 2020 (albeit further changes to the law are inevitable).

Keith Markham
June 2020

CONTENTS

PART A

FORCE MAJEURE

This section of the book sets out a summary of the key matters relating to the topic of force majeure. Each chapter focusses on a different issue and, having outlined the key content, concludes with a series of practical steps to be considered by the reader.

The chapters are as follows:

1. Introduction
2. Definition
3. Causation
4. Prevention and Mitigation
5. Notification and Termination
6. Trader to Consumer Contracts

CHAPTER ONE
INTRODUCTION

I had been expecting the e-mail but, when it came, I was a little surprised by the content which said something like:

> *'Why can't you understand that the government's order banning events is obviously force majeure. The courts will definitely agree with me so why can't you!'*

After allowing myself five minutes to take stock, I wrote back, pointing out some of the basic rules on force majeure clauses, and we managed to reach agreement as to a way forward.

In many ways, that e-mail encapsulates the dilemmas faced by many lawyers and their clients in dealing with problems caused by Covid-19. What does the clause actually say? should they insist on relying on that clause or should they adopt a more flexible approach?

The aim of this book is to provide a simple overview of the rules relating to force majeure and frustration and to consider what alternative approaches may be available. Particular emphasis will be placed on the applicability of these rules in the context of Covid-19.

1.1 Force majeure v frustration

There is no general principle of force majeure that applies to English contract law. However, it is open to the parties to any contract to insert such a clause which has the effect of excusing one of the parties from the performance of its obligations under the contract for a specific period of time. Only if that party is unable to resume performance, within a certain period of time, will the other party have the right to bring the contract to an end.

In the absence of such an express provision for the event that occurs, either party may rely on the doctrine of frustration. Frustration is said to occur:

> *"... whenever the law recognises that without default of either party a contractual obligation has become incapable of being performed because the circumstances in which performance is called for would render it a thing radically different from that which was undertaken by the contract. Non haec in foedera veni. It was not this that I promised to do."*[1]

If such a frustrating event were to occur, then further performance of the contract is rendered impossible and it is discharged with immediate effect. Unsurprisingly, the courts are reluctant to invoke such a doctrine lightly as will be discussed in more detail in chapter 7.

1.2 Key drafting considerations

When drafting a force majeure clause there are a number of key considerations that should be borne in mind:

- if you wish to rely on force majeure to excuse failure to perform under a contract there must be a clause dealing with this issue in the contract
- even if the contract does contain a force majeure clause then sometimes it may cover the event complained of and sometimes not – care should be taken as to what events are included or excluded
- a force majeure clause may contain a series of obligations that must be satisfied before it can be relied upon – this may include

1 Davis Contractors Ltd v. Fareham UDC, Lord Radcliffe [1956] 1 AC 696 at 729.

a requirement to notify the other party of any relevant force majeure event within a specified timeframe

- even if the force majeure clause does cover the force majeure event, there is still a general requirement to mitigate the effect of that event

All of these issues will be dealt with in more detail in later chapters, but it is important to note at the outset that when drafting a clause each party to the contract will have competing concerns which can be summarised as follows:

Customer (party assumed to have fewer obligations under the contract)	**Supplier (party assumed to have more obligations under the contract)**
Narrow definition of force majeure event	Broad definition of force majeure event
Exhaustive wording – specific list only	Non-exhaustive wording – 'including but not limited to …'
Narrow definition of impact – 'prevention'	Broad definition of impact – 'hinder, delay, prevent'
Formal notification required within a narrow timeframe	No formal notification requirement
Prevention requirement – 'could not have reasonably prevented …'	No prevention requirement
Mitigation requirement on Supplier	Minimal mitigation requirement

Requirement to resume performance as soon as reasonably practicable whether the force majeure event has ended or not	Limited requirement to resume performance – only when force majeure event has come to an end
Avoid reciprocal provision if possible	Reciprocal provision requiring Customer to mitigate effects as well
Only Customer can terminate	Either party to have the right to terminate
Short period of time before acquiring the right to terminate	Long period of time before acquiring the right to terminate

1.3 Relying on a force majeure clause

A contracting party will be able to rely on a force majeure clause to be excused from its obligations where it can establish the following:

- that the contract contains a force majeure clause that refers to the relevant event
- that the relevant event has occurred
- that the relevant event is the sole effective cause of the party's inability to perform its obligations
- that the relevant event was neither foreseeable nor preventable
- that the affected party took reasonable steps to mitigate the effect of the relevant event

- that the affected party notified the other contracting party of the relevant event in accordance with any specific notification requirements

If all these requirements can be satisfied, and performance cannot be resumed before the expiry of the time period specified in the force majeure clause, then the affected party may be entitled to terminate the contract.

All of these issues will be discussed in more detail in the following chapters.

1.4 Covid-19

I think that it is fair to say that many force majeure clauses are inserted into contracts without a great deal of thought. Some thought may have been directed to acts of God and government but specific references to epidemics and pandemics remain rare apart from in certain sectors. Then along came Covid-19 and suddenly these clauses were dusted down and every nuance of meaning was pored over hopefully (desperately?) in minute detail.

In this book I will examine how these clauses work and will go through the key issues referred to above. The main emphasis will be on Covid-19 but consideration will also be given to other potential force majeure events where appropriate.

1.5 Guidance

There are two documents that have now been published which may be of assistance:

Guidance on responsible contractual behaviour in the performance and enforcement of contracts impacted by the Covid-19 emergency

This document has been produced by the cabinet office. Published on the 7th May 2020, it sets out a series of suggestions in respect of 'responsible contractual behaviour' and can be accessed here:

https://www.gov.uk/government/publications/guidance-on-responsible-contractual-behaviour-in-the-performance-and-enforcement-of-contracts-impacted-by-the-covid-19-emergency

This document and its contents will be discussed in more detail in chapter 8.

Covid-19 – pandemic, consumer contracts, cancellation and refunds

This document was published by the Competition and Markets Authority ('CMA') on the 30th April 2020 and provides focussed, Covid-19 related guidance on issues such as cancellation and refunds in the context of Trader to Consumer contracts. It can be accessed here:

https://www.gov.uk/government/publications/cma-to-investigate-concerns-about-cancellation-policies-during-the-coronavirus-covid-19-pandemic/the-coronavirus-covid-19-pandemic-consumer-contracts-cancellation-and-refunds

This document and its contents will be discussed in more detail in chapter 6.

1.6 Trader to Consumer Contracts

One of the most controversial aspects as to how the Covid-19 outbreak has unfolded in the UK has been the extent to which a considerable number of traders have sought to rely on Covid-19 to cancel contracts with consumers, and refuse to provide refunds or to return deposits.

The CMA established a task force in respect of Covid-19 related matters on 20th March 2020 and produced the aforementioned guidance note shortly thereafter. As will be seen in chapter 6, the CMA's view is that traders should be providing refunds to consumers in almost all cases and it has already begun a formal investigation into those sectors where the worst abuses have taken place.

1.7 Summary

In summary, the Covid-19 outbreak has already had a profound impact on both our society and our economy. Its precise impact on our contracts remains to be seen, but in the meantime it is essential for all lawyers and their clients to familiarise themselves afresh with their force majeure clauses and consider how they can be used as either a shield or a sword.

CHAPTER TWO
DEFINITION

2.1 Introduction

The most important aspect of any force majeure clause is the way in which the phrase 'force majeure' or 'force majeure event' is defined. In English law there is no standard definition of 'force majeure'. Therefore, the parties have significant freedom to include or exclude a wide range of events and also to adopt an exhaustive or non-exhaustive approach to the way the clause applies. In this chapter, I will consider the three possible phrases that could refer to Covid-19 and will then set out two possible approaches to drafting that can be taken, as well as considering what sort of events would not normally be considered as amounting to force majeure.

2.2 Key phrases

There are three key phrases to look for in a force majeure clause which could cover recent events in respect of Covid-19. In this section I will summarise the law in respect of each in turn.

2.2.1 Epidemic and pandemic

Clearly the first thing to check in respect of a force majeure clause is whether it contains a specific reference to either 'epidemic' or 'pandemic'.

Epidemic can be defined as:[1]

> *A sudden increase in the number of cases of a disease—more than what's typically expected for the population in that area*

---

1 https://www.health.com/condition/infectious-diseases/epidemic-vs-pandemic

Pandemic can be defined as:

> *An epidemic that has spread over several countries or continents, affecting a large number of people*

It is important to note that the World Health Organisation declared that the Covid-19 outbreak was a pandemic on the 11th March 2020.

Of course, this information alone should not be treated as providing a 'get out of jail card' in respect of contracts from that date. The mere fact that an epidemic or pandemic exists does not of itself mean that a contracting party was unable to perform its obligations as a result of this. In subsequent chapters I will outline the importance of proving causation on a 'but for' basis, as well as demonstrating compliance with notification procedures and the need to mitigate the effect of the force majeure event and resume performance.

2.2.2 Act of God

This phrase has only been considered on a few occasions by the English courts and this has usually been in the context of a defence to negligence claims or in carriage contracts. The limited case law suggests that an act of God has the following characteristics:

(i) exclusively the consequence of natural causes[2]

In particular, this means that the act must involve *'elementary forces of nature unconnected with the agency of man or other cause'*[3]

Examples of acts of God from the case law include:

- storms[4]

---

2 Nugent v Smith [1876] 1 C.P.D. 423

3 Nugent v Smith [ibid]

4 Cushing v Peter Walker & Son [1941] 2 All ER 693

- flooding and lightning[5]
- heavy snowfall[6]

(ii) extraordinary or overwhelming[7]

The general consensus is that for a natural event to be extraordinary or overwhelming it must be unprecedented in scale. Examples from the case law include:

- unprecedented rainfall[8]
- extraordinarily high tide[9]
- extraordinary snowfall[10]
- extraordinary flood[11]

(iii) cannot be anticipated or provided against

In particular, the event must not have been capable of being *'prevented by any amount of foresight and pains and care reasonably expected'* by the contracting party seeking to rely on it.

The general consensus is that a contracting party cannot be expected to provide against an unprecedented event. The best example of this was a case where the court held that the defendant could have prevented loss

5 Forward v Pittard [1785] 99 E.R. 953

6 Briddon v Great North Railway Co. (1858) 28 LJ Ex 51

7 Nugent v Smith [supra]

8 Thomas v Birmingham Canal Co (1879) 49 LJQB 851

9 Nicols v Marsland [1876] 2 Ex.D.1

10 Briddon v Great North Railway Co. [supra]

11 Nicols v Marsland [supra]

from a flood by putting protective measures in place but could not reasonably be expected to prepare against an unprecedented flood.[12]

(iv) Application to Covid-19

As can be seen from the age of the cases referred to in this section, the issue of 'act of God' is not commonly discussed by the English courts. This is perhaps because, in more recent times, contracting parties tend to insert more detailed force majeure provisions that render discussions about 'acts of God' largely redundant.

As has been mentioned above, a contracting party relying on a force majeure clause would first consider whether there were specific references to 'epidemic', 'pandemic' or 'act of government' before then considering any 'including but not limited to' references. Only then would they be likely to fall back on 'act of God' if they had no other choice.

Nevertheless, reliance on 'act of God' could be raised as a valid argument and I shall now consider how this might apply in the context of Covid-19.

(a) exclusively the consequence of natural causes

First, we must consider whether the inability to perform under the contract was due to Covid-19 itself or actions taken by the government in response to the Covid-19. This is likely to depend on the extent of the lockdown measures introduced in a given country. If the failure to perform was because employees fell ill and were unable to work then then there are some cases that suggest that a disease, such as Covid-19, can fall within the concept of 'act of God'.[13] However, if the failure to perform was due the lockdown measures that were introduced then it is less likely that act of God could be relied upon.

---

12 Nicols v Marsland [supra]

13 Boast v Firth [1868-69] L.R. 4 C.P. 1; Ryan v Youngs [1938] 1 All ER 522

(b) extraordinary or overwhelming

Given the unprecedented speed with which Covid-19 spread globally it is quite possible that this limb of the test may be satisfied, subject to the comments in (a) above.

(c) cannot be anticipated or provided against

Clearly there have been outbreaks of similar diseases before – for example SARS in 2003 and therefore it could be argued that steps could have been taken to prevent a similar global spread of disease. The response to this would be that such steps could only realistically be implemented with the cooperation of the World Health Organisation and national governments. Given the lack of cooperation there, arguably, was little that a contracting party could have done.

(v) Summary

In summary, there are clearly some good arguments in favour of relying on 'act of God' but my preference would be to try and rely on some of the other events that are discussed elsewhere in this chapter wherever possible.

2.2.3 Act of Government

The next issue to be considered is whether Covid-19 has led to certain 'acts of government' that could constitute a force majeure event. To that end it is necessary to consider what legislation has been enacted within the UK and what effect this has had.

Please note that in this book I will consider the effects of the relevant legislation in England only. As readers will be aware, at the beginning of the crisis a uniform approach was typically adopted but more recently there had been increasing divergence and it is beyond the scope of this book to chronicle every nuance.

(i) Coronavirus Act 2020

The Coronavirus Act 2020 ('the Act') came into force on 25th March 2020 and a summary of its content is set out in appendix 1. It can be accessed here:

http://www.legislation.gov.uk/ukpga/2020/7/contents

The key provisions to note are as follows:

(a) Definitions[14]

Term	Definition
"coronavirus"	means severe acute respiratory syndrome coronavirus 2 (SARS-CoV-2);
"coronavirus disease"	means COVID-19 (the official designation of the disease which can be caused by coronavirus).

(b) Duration

The Act expires at the end of the period of two years beginning with the day on which it was passed[15]. However, this period can be extended in certain circumstances.[16]

14 s1(1) Coronavirus Act 2020

15 s89 CA 2020

16 s90 CA 2020

(c) Powers relating to events, gatherings and premises

This issue is dealt with in s52 and schedule 22 of the Act. In particular, schedule 22 part 2 contains provisions in respect of the following matters pertaining to England:

Para No(s).	Provision
3-4	Declaration of threat to public health in England due to coronavirus
5	Power to prohibit or otherwise restrict events or gatherings in England
6	Power to close premises in England or impose restrictions on persons entering or remaining in them
7	Variations and revocations
8	Procedure for issuing directions in consultation with the chief medical officer
9-10	Offences
11	Enforcements and prosecutions
12	End of public health response period

The Act is then supplemented with a considerable number of statutory instruments but the most relevant for our purposes is:

(ii) The Health Protection (Coronavirus, Restrictions) (England) Regulations 2020 ('the Regulations')

The Regulations came into force on 26th March 2020 and have since been updated on 22nd April 2020[17], 13th May 2020[18] and 1st June 2020 respectively.[19] They revoked the Health Protection (Coronavirus, Business Closure) (England) Regulations 2020 that had been in place previously.

(a) Duration

The Regulations are stated to expire six months from the date that they came into force[20] and the government is required to review the Regulations at least once every twenty-one days.[21]

(b) Key Provisions

During the 'emergency period'[22] the following requirements must be followed:

- businesses listed in parts 1 and 2 of schedule 2 must be closed[23]

---

17 The Health Protection (Coronavirus, Restrictions) (England) (Amendment) Regulations 2020 http://www.legislation.gov.uk/uksi/2020/447/contents/made

18 The Health Protection (Coronavirus, Restrictions) (England) (Amendment) (No. 2) Regulations 2020 http://www.legislation.gov.uk/uksi/2020/500/contents/made

19 The Health Protection (Coronavirus, Restrictions) (England) (Amendment) (No. 3) Regulations 2020 http://www.legislation.gov.uk/uksi/2020/558/pdfs/uksi_20200558_en.pdf

20 Regulation 12(1)

21 Regulation 3(2) – first review date was 16th April 2020

22 This is defined in Regulation 3(1) as beginning on the date the Regulations came into force and ending in respect of a specific requirement or restriction when directed by the Secretary of State

23 Regulation 4

- businesses listed in part 3 of schedule 2 may remain open subject to certain restrictions[24]

Furthermore, the Regulations set out restrictions on movement[25] and gatherings[26] with which we are all familiar.

A full summary of the content of the Regulations is set out in appendix 2. The Regulations are also accessible here:

http://www.legislation.gov.uk/uksi/2020/350/contents

Further changes are expected in due course and therefore lawyers and their clients need to keep up to date in respect of which activities are permitted and which businesses are allowed to open at a given time. This will be particularly important when considering issues concerning the calculation of time period in respect of notification and termination referred to in chapter 5.

(iii) Covid-19

If a contracting party is unable to perform its obligations due to the government prohibiting certain activity such as gatherings of a certain size or the enforced closure of a specific business then this is likely to constitute an act of government and therefore could be relied upon as a force majeure event. However, where a contracting party decided to close voluntarily then they will not be able to rely on 'act of Government'. Therefore, care should be taken to consider when the Regulations referred to above came into force and whether failure to perform was due to the Regulations or due to the contracting party's voluntary decision. Furthermore, the same warning about 'get out of jail cards' applies equally in respect of this potential force majeure event.

---

24 Regulation 5

25 Regulation 6

26 Regulation 7

2.3 Different approaches

There are two possible ways of structuring the definition of 'force majeure' in a clause. First, this can be done on an exhaustive basis whereby force majeure is limited solely to specific events that are listed. The alternative is, unsurprisingly, to do this on a non-exhaustive basis. In this case, a list of events is provided but the clause also includes a phrase such as 'including without limitation' which suggests that other events may also be caught.

The former approach tends towards a narrower interpretation and the latter towards a broader interpretation. As was mentioned in chapter 1, the parties to the contract are likely to have different views as to which of these approaches to adopt.

I will now set out an example of each approach and will consider the extent to which Covid-19 would fall within the wording.

2.3.1 Exhaustive definition

An exhaustive definition would typically be structured in the following way:

> *"Force Majeure Event" means any exceptional event or circumstance being:*
>
> - *any act of God;*
> - *war or threat of war, armed conflict, sabotage, terrorist attack, insurrection, riot, civil disturbance or requisition;*
> - *fire;*
> - *earthquake;*
> - *explosion;*

- *nuclear, chemical or biological contamination;*
- *epidemic or pandemic;*
- *an overt political act that directly causes a Party material delay or an inability to perform its obligations hereunder;*
- *act of government;*
- *extreme adverse weather conditions;*

Therefore, if the event is not referred to on this list it could not be relied upon to excuse a contracting party from its obligations.

In this case, there are clear references to 'act of God', 'epidemic' and 'pandemic' which would suggest that Covid-19 would potentially be covered. Alternatively, the phrase 'act of government' could potentially cover actions taken by the government[27] in the light of Covid-19 which meant that a contracting party could not fulfil their obligations.

Of course, whether that contracting party could rely on one or more of these events to be excused from performing their obligations under the contract would be subject to causation, notification and timing issues which are discussed in more detail in later chapters.

2.3.2 Non-exhaustive definition

The alternative approach would typically be structured in one of the following ways (key words highlighted):

> *'A Force Majeure Event* ***shall include, but not be limited*** *to flood, storm, fire, war, terrorist act, riot, strike or other industrial action, breakdown of machinery, shortages of materials, or a delay or failure*

27 For example, as set out in the Health Protection (Coronavirus, Restrictions) (England) Regulations 2020 (as amended)

> *on the part of any sub-contractor, supplier or carrier of goods or materials relating to this Agreement.'*
>
> *Force Majeure Event*
>
> *'acts, events, omissions or non-events beyond its reasonable control,* ***including*** *riots, war, acts of terrorism, fire, flood, storm or earthquake and any disaster, but excluding any industrial dispute relating to the Supplier, the Supplier's Personnel or any other failure in the Supplier's supply chain'*

In both these clauses there is no specific reference to 'epidemic', 'pandemic', 'act of God' or 'act of government'. Consequently, a party seeking to be excused from their obligations under either of these clauses would need to establish that Covid-19 fell within the reference to *'shall include, but not be limited to'* or *'including'*.

Previous case law suggests that so-called 'sweeper' wording of the sort referred to above will typically be given its wider and natural meaning and will not usually be limited to categories of events either preceding or following the phrase.[28] In practice, this would mean that Covid-19 may be covered under phrases such as *'including but not limited to …'*. However, more recent case law suggest that this may not always be the case.

2.3.3 Applicable case law

Further guidance on the usage of 'sweeper' wording may be obtained from the case of **Tandrin v Aero Toy Store**[29]

In this case, the parties entered into a contract for the sale by Tandrin to ATS of a new Bombardier executive aircraft for the sum of $31.75

28 Chandris v Isbrandtsen-Moller Co Inc [1951] 1 KB 240

29 [2010] EWHC 40 (Comm) Hamblen J

million. ATS paid a deposit of $3 million to an escrow agent which was due to be released to Tandrin, together with the balance, when the aircraft was delivered.

Tandrin purchased the aircraft from its original owner for $26.5 million and then sought to deliver it to ATS. ATS refused to accept delivery and did not pay the balance of the purchase price, furthermore they did not instruct the escrow agent to release the deposit. Tandrin then sold the aircraft to another party for $24.5 million and sought to recover their losses from ATS alleging breach of contract.

The contract contained the following force majeure clause:

> *'Force Majeure. Neither party shall be liable to the other as a result of any failure of, or delay in the performance of, its obligations hereunder, for the period that such failure or delay is due to: Acts of God or the public enemy; war, insurrection or riots; fires; governmental actions; strikes or labor disputes; inability to obtain aircraft materials, accessories, equipment or parts from vendors;* ***or any other cause beyond Seller's reasonable control.'***

ATS argued that they were entitled to reject delivery of the aircraft because the "*unanticipated, unforeseeable and cataclysmic downward spiral of the world's financial markets*" triggered the force majeure clause in the Agreement, thereby postponing the time for ATS to complete the purchase and potentially affecting the price at which ATS should be entitled to purchase the Aircraft.

Tandrin countered that an economic downturn had never been held to be force majeure in English law and the proposal by ATS to postpone purchase until it was commercially reasonable was unworkable in practice.

High Court Decision

The judge found in favour of Tandrin and dismissed ATS's arguments relating to force majeure. In particular, he noted that:

- it was well-established under English law that a change in economic or market circumstances did not constitute a force majeure event; and

- the term 'force majeure' was not a term of art and whether a force majeure clause was triggered depended on the proper construction of the wording of the clause in each case;

He then proceeded to analyse the meaning of the phrase ***'any other cause beyond the Seller's reasonable control'*** and made the following observations:

- the phrase needed to be read in the context of the entire clause

- none of the other phrases in the clause were even remotely connected to issues relating to an economic downturn

- the clause only referred to matters beyond the seller's (Tandrin's) control and did not refer to matters beyond the buyer's (ATS's) control

- therefore, the natural and ordinary meaning of the clause was that it was a clause that only the seller (Tandrin) could rely upon and this was further supported by the fact that the seller had the majority of the obligations under the contract

- the clause could not sensibly be construed to cover matters that the seller was not concerned with (eg financing arrangements)

- furthermore, to construe the clause as if it were worded 'any other cause beyond the purchaser's control or 'any other cause beyond either party's control' would be wrong because it would fundamentally alter the meaning of the phrase and would give no meaning to the words 'the seller's'

In conclusion he noted that:

- instead the expression should be construed to comprise only those matters which have some connection with the seller's obligations under the Agreement and/or with which the seller would have been expected to be concerned

Interestingly, he then proceeded to provide the following example:

For instance, matters relevant to the delivery of the aircraft (which is the obligation of the seller and a matter principally under the seller's control) would be caught by that clause, such as the seller being unable to deliver the aircraft on time due to a pandemic causing a dearth of delivery pilots.

2.3.4 Summary

In the light of this case, it is clear that each clause will need to be considered on its merits and whether a specific event like Covid-19 will be caught is by no means guaranteed. However, the example given by the judge in Tandrin does suggest that the effects of Covid-19 could well be said to be a force majeure event that did prevent a contracting party from performing its obligations, even when the clause does not specifically refer to it.

2.4 Additional considerations

In addition to the points discussed so far in this chapter, there are two other matters that are of note when drafting a force majeure clause.

2.4.1 Matters excluded

As has already been mentioned, certain types of event are typically regarded by the courts as not being examples of force majeure. However, such matters may be inserted expressly into a force majeure clause and therefore care should be taken when drafting the clause depending on the viewpoint of each contracting party. Common examples of matters that should either be removed from such a clause or expressly excluded are:

- strikes or industrial disputes relating to the employees of one of the parties
- breakdown of machinery
- shortages of materials
- delay or failure on the part of any sub-contractor, supplier or carrier of goods or materials relating to this Agreement.

2.4.2 Industry specific matters

Another consideration to be borne in mind is that additional force majeure events may need to be added to a clause in respect of industry specific matters. Often there can be a temptation to rely on the 'usual suspects' when drafting such a clause but parties would be well-advised to think about specific additional instances. For example, in the context of a shipping contract the following matters might be added to the definition of force majeure:

- breaking off of diplomatic relations;
- import or export regulations, sanctions, quotas, restrictions, embargoes or failure to be granted relevant licences or consents;
- loss at sea;

- extreme adverse weather conditions;
- the restriction of vessel traffic imposed by the Port Authority for any reason into or out of the Container Terminal;

2.5 Summary

In summary, the definition of force majeure in each contract needs to be considered on its merits. In the context of Covid-19 the key phrases to look out for remain 'epidemic', 'pandemic' and 'act of government' albeit 'act of God' should not be entirely ruled out. Of course, if none of the above are available, it is possible that Covid-19 might just be included under a reference to 'including but not limited to' or 'other cause beyond the control of the parties' but the courts interpret these statements carefully as has been discussed.

However, the identification of a force majeure event referred to in a given clause is not the end of the matter, rather it is the beginning of further arguments about causation and other matters that will be discussed in the next few chapters.

2.6 Practical steps

It is assumed that the supplier will have more obligations under the contract than the customer and therefore will seek to draft a clause that allows greater possibilities to be excused from their obligations under force majeure.

Customer

- draft a clause that has a narrower range of force majeure events

- remove any events that would not normally be considered as examples of force majeure
- limit references to 'including but not limited to'
- limit references to 'beyond reasonable control' to events that are beyond its own reasonable control only

Supplier

- draft a clause that includes a wide range of force majeure events
- add any sector specific events that might not otherwise be included
- add references to 'including but not limited to' if possible
- ensure that any reference to 'beyond reasonable control' covers events that are beyond its own reasonable control

CHAPTER THREE
CAUSATION

3.1 Introduction

Having established that a force majeure event has happened, it is then necessary to establish causation between that event and the inability of the contracting party to perform its obligations. Unsurprisingly, this issue has been discussed frequently by the courts. In this chapter, I will outline the basic principles from existing case law, and will then consider the wording relating to causation that is typically found in force majeure clauses.

3.2 Basic principles

The issue of causation has been discussed in three recent cases and I set out below a brief summary of each case and the principles that have emerged from them.

Tandrin v Aero Toy Store

The facts of this case have already been discussed in chapter 2 so will not be reprised here. In short, the court made the following key observations relating to causation:

- the phrase 'a cause beyond the Seller's reasonable control' should be construed as only covering matters which would have a causal link with the performance of the seller's own obligations

- therefore, clause 7.17 required a causal link between 'the cause beyond the seller's reasonable control' and the failure / delay in the performance of the obligation

- in this case there was no such causal link between the inability of the seller to influence or control the credit markets and purchaser's inability to pay the purchase price

These issues were considered more recently in the case of:

Seadrill Ghana Operations Limited v Tullow Ghana Limited[1]

Tullow Ghana Limited had interests in two offshore petroleum licences or concessions about 60kms off the coast of Ghana, namely the TEN Field and the Greater Jubilee Field. In 2012 it entered into a long-term drilling contract with Seadrill for the hire of a semi-submersible drilling rig 'West Leo' to be used for offshore drilling. The daily operating rate was $600,000 and the contract was due to expire in 2018.

The contract contained the following force majeure clauses:

Section 2A Clause 27

> *27.1 Neither COMPANY nor CONTRACTOR shall be responsible for any failure to fulfil any term or condition of the Contract if and to the extent that fulfilment has been delayed or temporarily prevented by an occurrence, as hereunder defined as FORCE MAJEURE, which has been notified in accordance with this Clause 27 and which is beyond the control and without the fault or negligence of the party affected and which, by the exercise of reasonable diligence, the said party is unable to prevent or provide against. Both parties shall use their reasonable endeavours to mitigate, avoid, circumvent, or overcome the circumstances of FORCE MAJEURE."*
>
> *27.2 For the purpose of the Contract, Force majeure shall be limited to the following:*
>
> …………

1 [2018] EWHC 1640 (Comm) Teare J

> *(h) Drilling moratorium imposed by the government*
>
> ....
>
> *27.5 In the event of force majeure occurrence, the party that is or may be delayed in performing the Contract shall notify the other party without delay giving the full particulars thereof and shall use all reasonable endeavours to remedy the situation without delay.*
>
> ....
>
> *27.8 In the event that a FORCE MAJEURE condition prevails for a period of sixty (60) consecutive days then COMPANY may terminate the CONTRACT forthwith by giving notice, or may elect keeping CONTRACTOR under CONTRACT and keep paying the DAILY FORCE MAJEURE RATE.'*

Tullow envisaged that West Leo would be used, first of all, in the TEN Field and would subsequently be used in the Greater Jubilee Field.

In 2015 a dispute arose between Cote d'Ivoire and Ghana as to precisely where the offshore boundary lay between them. If Cote d'Ivoire were correct, then the TEN Field would lie within their territorial waters. The dispute was referred to the International Tribunal for the Law of the Sea which decided to grant a Provisional Measures Order ('PMO') in April 2015 stating that:

'Ghana shall take all necessary steps to ensure that no new drilling either by Ghana or under its control takes place in the disputed area'

As a result of this decision, the Ghanaian government issued a letter in May 2015 stating that existing work in the TEN Field could be completed but that no new wells could be 'spudded' (i.e. the process of drilling an initial hole in the seabed).

At that time, Tullow's drilling schedule still anticipated that West Leo would be used to complete work in the TEN Field until October 2016 and would then be re-deployed to the Greater Jubilee Field.

Subsequently, in 2016, the following events occurred:

February 2016

The Ghanaian government refused to approve further drilling in the Greater Jubilee Field which meant that West Leo could not be used there in due course

15th March 2016

Tullow wrote to Seadrill advising it of *"events which may result in Force Majeure...... which may prevent Work from being performed in Ghana".*

Tullow referred to the PMO and to the Ghanaian Government's subsequent letter. Tullow said that the Government had "rejected" the Greater Jubilee Plan and that Tullow was working to understand and respond to the reasons for the rejection and to seek approval for further drilling.

They then concluded that:

> *"Given, however, the rejection of the Jubilee Development Plan, drilling must de facto cease within the Jubilee field area. As things currently stand, therefore, it is no longer possible to conduct Jubilee field work under the Drilling Contract. It is [Tullow's] position that the above both individually and cumulatively may result in Force Majeure ....which may prevent Work from being performed in Ghana. Based upon our current estimates, if unresolved, the Force majeure occurrences will mean that drilling activity will cease around 3 October 2016."*

1st September 2016

On this date, Tullow gave notice of a force majeure occurrence to occur on or around the 5th October 2016 when the 'moratorium on drilling with the TEN Field will arise'

Tullow concluded that it would be unable to fulfil its obligations under the contract due to the PMO, the Government's instruction and the rejection of the Greater Jubilee Plan which *'either individually and/or cumulatively, give rise to a Force majeure occurrence'.*

1st October 2016

Work ended on the last well in the TEN Field and Tullow confirmed that the Force Majeure was in effect.

10th November 2016

West Leo left Ghanaian waters for storage in the Canary Islands.

1st December 2016

Tullow advised Seadrill that the contract was terminated pursuant to clause 27.8 as the moratorium had continued for 60 days.

Submissions of the Parties

Tullow argued that the cause of its failure to comply with its obligations under the contract in October 2016 was a force majeure event, namely the drilling moratorium imposed by the Government of Ghana.

Seadrill agreed that the drilling moratorium imposed by the Government of Ghana was, prima facie, a force majeure event but disputed that this was the sole cause of Tullow's inability to perform its obligations. Instead they argued that the primary cause was in face the

Ghanaian government's refusal to approve further drilling in the Greater Jubilee Field.

High Court Decision

Teare J considered the arguments of the parties and made the following observations concerning the issue of causation:

- clause 27.1 of the contract required Tullow to have been prevented from or delayed in fulfilling its obligations by an occurrence which was a force majeure.

- consequently there was a clear causation requirement between the force majeure and Tullow's failure to provide drilling instructions to Seadrill

- questions of causation were sensitive to the legal context in which they arose

- however, such questions should be resolved by taking a *'broad common sense view of the whole position'*

He then proceeded to consider the facts of the case and noted that:

- there were two effective causes of Tullow being unable to provide drilling instructions in October 2016, namely the drilling moratorium affecting the TEN Field and the decision of the Ghanaian government not to approve further drilling in the Greater Jubilee Field

- the former was a force majeure event, and the latter was not

- therefore, the question arose as to whether, on the true construction of clause 27, Tullow could show that it was delayed in or prevented from doing so by a force majeure event

- in particular, Tullow were required to show that the force majeure event was the sole cause of their failure to perform their obligations

In reaching his conclusion, the judge also bore in mind evidence of a plan by Tullow to manipulate the force majeure clause as a means of ending what had become, for them, an unprofitable contract. Tellingly employees of Tullow had exchanged e-mails referring to 'Project Voldemort' which evidenced:

> *"an understanding amongst some members of the team that force majeure may be an option for a possible route for going ahead in this situation we found ourselves."*

and that:

> *'with a bit of manipulation it was possible to use the PMO to call force majeure on ... the West Leo"*

Of course, the judge also took the opportunity to note that:

> *'In the "Harry Potter" novels Lord Voldemort is, so I was informed, an evil and destructive character.'*

Albeit he did not recall that the usual convention is to refer to him as 'he who must not be named'.

Taking all these matters into consideration the judge concluded that:[2]

- clause 27.1 contained a causation requirement in these terms: "if and to the extent that fulfilment has been delayed or temporarily prevented by an occurrence, as hereunder defined as Force Majeure"

2 Paragraph 78

- Tullow had intended to drill and complete wells in the Greater Jubilee Field from October 2016.

- that intention was not frustrated by a force majeure event but by an event which was not a force majeure event, namely, the failure of the Government to approve the Greater Jubilee Plan.

- Tullow's own intention with regard to drilling in the Greater Jubilee Field in October 2016 had also changed

- thus, with regard to the Greater Jubilee Field, a force majeure event did not to any extent delay or prevent Tullow from drilling there in October 2016.

- Tullow was unable to rely upon the force majeure clause notwithstanding that the force majeure event prevented it from using West Leo to complete one specific well in the TEN Field

- any other conclusion would mean that Tullow could terminate the contract pursuant to clause 27 where the effective cause of its failure to perform was not a force majeure event within the meaning of the clause.

Finally, we need to consider the case of:

Classic Maritime v Limbungan[3]

Classic Maritime entered into a contract of affreightment ('COA') for the carriage of iron ore pellets from Brazil to Malaysia. Limbungan, a Malaysian company, was the charterer under the COA. The COA contained the following force majeure clause:

3 [2018] EWHC 2389 (Comm) Teare J; [2019] EWCA Civ 1102 Males LJ

> *"EXCEPTIONS Neither the Vessel, her Master or Owners, nor the Charterers, Shippers or Receivers shall be Responsible for loss or damage to, or failure to supply, load, discharge or deliver the cargo* ***resulting From:*** *Act of God, act of war, act of public enemies, pirates or assailing thieves; arrest or restraint of princes, rulers or people; embargoes; seizure under legal process, provided bond is promptly Furnished to release the Vessel or cargo; floods; frosts; fogs; fires; epidemics; quarantine; Intervention of sanitary, customs or other constituted authorities; Blockades; Blockages; riots; insurrections; civil commotions; political disturbances; earthquakes; Landslips; explosions; collisions; strandings, and accidents of navigation;* ***accidents at the mine*** *or Production facility or to machinery or to loading equipment; accidents at the Receivers' works, Port, wharf or facility; or any other causes beyond the Owners', Charterers', Shippers' or Receivers' Control; always provided that any such events* ***directly affect the performance*** *of either party under This Charter Party."*

On 5 November 2015, the Fundao dam, in the industrial complex of Germano in Brazil where iron ore was mined, burst. Slurry flowed down to the Atlantic Ocean swamping villages in its wake. The bursting of the dam also stopped production at the nearby iron ore mine.

Limbungan argued that the bursting of the dam was a force majeure event which prevented them from performing their obligations under the COA. Furthermore, they submitted that while the clause imposed a causation requirement in the sense that it had to be shown that the dam burst rendered performance of its obligations impossible, it was not necessary for it to show also that, but for the dam burst, it would have performed its obligations.

Classic Maritime accepted that the bursting of the dam fell within the phrase 'accidents at the mine' however they argued that clause 32 imported a causation requirement by the use of the words 'resulting from' and by the requirement that the force majeure must directly affect the performance of Limbungan's obligations. They argued that Limbungan's failure to perform did not result from this event nor had the events directly affected Limbungan's performance. They claimed damages in the sum of $20 million in respect of five shipments which should have taken place after the dam had burst.

High Court Decision

Teare J made the following important observations:

- everything depended upon the wording of the particular clause.

- in this case clause 32 imported a causation requirement by the use of the words "resulting from" and by the requirement that the force majeure must "directly affect" the performance of Limbungan's obligations.

- the judge quoted approvingly from his decision in Seadrill (see above) and emphasised the need to apply a broad common-sense view of the whole position

- to do this he applied the "reasonable and realistic businessman" test[4] and considered that such a businessman would see the broad common sense of saying that if, but for the dam burst, Limbungan would not have performed its obligations, its failure to perform could not fairly be said to have "resulted from" the dam burst and the dam burst could not fairly be said to have "directly affected" the performance of Limbungan's obligations.

- the important factual issue therefore was whether, but for the dam burst, Limbungan would have supplied cargo for the 5 voyages between November 2015 and June 2016 which were the subject of the present claim.

---

4 The Furness Bridge [1977] 2 Lloyd's Reports 367 – Kerr J

- this was bound up with the question as to whether Limbungan had made any "relevant arrangements" (para 90) and the burden of proof on this issue lay on Limbungan.

He then proceeded to consider the evidence and ruled that Limbungan had not discharged the burden of proof and were therefore unable to rely on the force majeure clause. Limbungan appealed to the Court of Appeal.

Court of Appeal Decision

The leading judgement was given by Males LJ who upheld the decision of the High Court and made the following additional comments in respect of force majeure:

- the purpose of clause 32 was to be gathered from its terms

- the citation of cases with differently worded clauses was of limited value

- the words "resulting from" together with the requirement that the events in question "directly affect the performance of either party" imported a causation requirement.

- the High Court was correct to say that a reasonable and realistic businessman would see the broad common sense of saying that if, but for the dam burst, Limbungan would not have performed its obligations, its failure to perform could not fairly be said to have 'resulted from' the dam burst and the dam burst could fairly be said to have 'directly affected' the performance of Limbungan's obligations

- when deciding whether Limbungan could rely on clause 32 in circumstances where it would not have performed its obligation anyway, what mattered was not how the clause was labelled but the language of the clause

In the light of these cases the following points should be noted:

- the party seeking to rely on the force majeure clause must establish a causative link between the force majeure event and its inability to perform its obligations
- furthermore, the force majeure event must be the sole effective cause
- the courts will apply a 'but for' test when determining this
- the courts will also apply a broad common-sense approach and ask what a 'reasonable and realistic businessman' would think
- if there are a number of possible causes, the courts are less likely to allow a party to rely on a force majeure clause

3.3 Drafting considerations

As has been discussed above, the party seeking to rely on the force majeure clause to be excused from performing its obligations will have to establish a causal link. However, as has also been seen, each clause tends to deal with the extent of the inability to perform in a different way.

I set out below a series of possible variations and comments as to their desirability:

3.3.1 Failure to perform

Subject to the following provisions of this clause 21, ***neither party*** *shall be considered to be in default of this Agreement or liable to the other party by reason of any* ***failure*** *in the performance of that party's obligations under this Agreement* ***if caused*** *by* ***any*** *act, omission or circumstance* ***beyond the reasonable control of that party***

This clause is relatively simplistic and contains the following elements:

- both parties are entitled to rely upon it
- the impact of the force majeure is limited to 'failure' only and therefore does not include scenarios where a party is delayed, prevented or hindered
- the words 'if caused' establish a clear requirement for causation
- the reference to 'any act etc beyond the reasonable control of that party' suggest a wide definition of force majeure

3.3.2 Prevention, delay or hindrance

> *... in the event that either party is* ***delayed or prevented from or hindered*** *in performing its obligations under this agreement by a Force Majeure Event ...*

This clause is more favourable to the party seeking to be excused as it widens the scenarios in which the clause applies to include prevention, delay and hindrance.

(i) Prevention

Prevention is said to include:

- 'physical or legal prevention' and not merely economic unprofitability[5]

However, it will not include the following scenarios:

- an obligation to supply becomes 'commercially unacceptable or impracticable'[6]

- where goods can be obtained from another supplier[7]

(ii) Delay

There is no specific definition of this available from the case law. However, it should be treated differently from 'prevent' or 'hinder' and the clause may provide for an extension of time for performance in such circumstances.

(iii) Hinder

This phrase provides the greatest amount of flexibility to a party seeking to be excused from its obligations. Case law suggest that 'hinder' means:

'an interference with the manufacture or delivery from the same cause as 'preventing', but interference of a less degree'[8]

On the facts of that case the court held that:

'to place a merchant in the position of being unable to deliver unless he dislocates his business and breaks his contracts in order to fulfil one surely hinders delivery'

---

5 Tennants (Lancashire) Ltd v G S Wilson & Co Ltd [1917] AC 495

6 Dunavant Enterprises Inc v Olympia Spinning [2011] 2 Lloyd's Rep 619

7 Hoecheong Products Co Ltd v Cargill Hong Kong Ltd [1995] 1 WLR 404

8 Tennants (Lancashire) Ltd [supra]

However, the court also noted that a simple rise in price, which made the contract more expensive to carry out, would not in itself be a hindrance.

(iv) Summary

Clearly a party wishing to be excused from its obligations would be happy to include a reference to 'prevent, delay or hinder' while a party wishing to limit such possibilities would try and remove such phrases.

3.3.3 Extent of impact

Normally, a force majeure clause will refer to failure to perform a party's obligations under the agreement. This would typically be interpreted to mean failure to perform **any** of the obligations rather than failure to perform all of the obligations.

However, an alternative formulation could be as follows:

> *... a party is unable to perform a substantial part of its obligations under the agreement...*

There is no case law relating to the correct interpretation of such a provision. However, it is arguable that such a phrase would only allow a party to rely on the force majeure clause in circumstances where the force majeure event prevented that party from performing a significant percentage of its obligations thereby making it more difficult to rely on such a clause.

3.3.4 Extent of causation

It is commonly the case that a clause will refer to *'delay or failure arising from circumstances beyond the reasonable control of either party.'*

However, an alternative formulation could be as follows:

> *... if caused* ***in whole or in part*** *by circumstances beyond the reasonable control of either party.'*

As has previously been discussed the party seeking to rely on a force majeure clause will be required to show that the force majeure was the sole effective cause of its inability to perform its obligations. The wording used in this clause is potentially problematic for two reasons:

- the reference to 'in whole' effectively raises the bar on causation so that the force majeure event must be the sole cause rather than the sole effective cause thereby making it more difficult for it to be relied upon

- the reference to 'in part' effectively lowers the bar on causation so that the force majeure event does not need to be the sole effective cause

Clearly, both of these approaches are likely to be objected to by one of the contracting parties and therefore this phrase should be avoided.

3.4 Covid-19

In order to rely on force majeure in respect of Covid-19 a contracting party will need to establish a causal link. The following specific issues need to be considered:

3.4.1 Disease

In order to rely on any of the phrases 'epidemic', pandemic' or 'act of God' that appeared in the force majeure clause it would be necessary to show that the disease itself was the sole effective cause. This would likely require evidence that a certain percentage of employees became ill themselves with Covid-19 or were required to self-isolate because a member of their family was ill with Covid-19 or were deemed to be vulnerable. This could also apply where a key supplier or transport provider was affected in a similar way which meant that items could not be produced or transported in time.

3.4.2 Act of Government

Assuming that the phrase 'act of Government' appeared in the force majeure clause, the party wishing to rely on this it would need to show that the act of Government itself was the sole effective cause. As was discussed in chapter 2, the Government has introduced a series of restrictions which have meant that certain businesses have not been able to operate in the same way as before. If the inability to perform is solely due to this, the provision may well be triggered. However, if a business took a voluntary decision to close without a legal requirement being in force then this would not amount to a force majeure event until such time as the law made closure compulsory.

3.4.3 Wording of the clause

Of course, in both cases it would be important to consider whether the relevant clause referred to 'prevent', 'delay' or 'hinder'. Obviously, it would be far easier to establish that either the disease or the act of Government had hindered a party in the performance of its contractual obligations.

3.5 Summary

In summary, the courts have made it clear in recent cases that causation is of great importance when deciding whether a party can rely on force majeure to be excused from its obligations under a contract. However, it is also important to review and revise the wording of such clauses carefully as each clause will be interpreted on its merits by the courts.

3.6 Practical steps

Customer

- ensure that the clause has a clear causation requirement
- limit the extent of the clause's application to 'failure' or 'delay'
- consider adding a reference to 'a substantial part of its obligations'
- avoid references to 'in part'

Supplier

- ensure that the causation requirement is not unduly onerous
- add references to 'prevention' and 'hindrance'
- avoid references to 'a substantial part of its obligations'
- avoid references to 'in whole'

CHAPTER FOUR
PREVENTION AND MITIGATION

4.1 Introduction

Having established that there is a causal link between the force majeure event and the inability to perform its obligations, a party seeking to rely on the clause will next have to consider issues of prevention and mitigation. In this chapter I will set out the key concerns relating to these two issues and will also discuss potential wording.

4.2 Prevention

4.2.1 Guidance from case law

Questions of prevention are typically bound up with the issue of foreseeability and this issue was discussed at length in the following case:

2 Entertain Video Limited v Sony DADC Europe Limited[1]

Sony provided logistics services including warehousing and distribution of home entertainment media. The parties entered into an agreement for such services in May 2011.

Clause 14.1 of the agreement stated:

> *"Neither party shall be liable for its failure or delay in performing any of its obligations hereunder if such failure or delay is caused by circumstances beyond the reasonable control of the party affected including but not limited to industrial action (at either party), fire,*

---

1 [2020] EWHC 972 (TCC) O'Farrell J

flood, wars, armed conflict, terrorist act, riot, civil commotion, malicious damage, explosion, unavailability of fuel, pandemic or governmental or other regulatory action."

On the night of Monday 8th August 2011, a distribution warehouse operated by Sony was attacked by a group of young men, as part of the rioting and civil disorder that took place in London following the death of Mark Duggan. They gained access by breaking a fire door or glazed panels in the south west corner of the building. Having looted some of the goods contained therein they started a fire which lasted for ten days and caused the total destruction of the warehouse, including stock belonging to 2 Entertain valued at approximately £40million.

Sony's insurers paid out £8,270,573.37 in respect of the stock but 2 Entertain sought to recover additional losses either under an indemnity contained in the agreement or by way of damages. Sony disputed the claim on a number of grounds but I will focus on arguments relating to the force majeure clause.

High Court Decision

The judge began by considering whether Sony had taken reasonable measures to secure the warehouse and whether they had put in place reasonable fire precautions. Her conclusion was that Sony had failed in both respects.

Against this background she proceeded to consider the application of the force majeure clause and made the following observations:

- it was common ground that the riots were unforeseen and unprecedented
- however, the risk of intruders was foreseeable because unauthorised entry had been attempted and/or achieved during incidents that occurred prior to the riot.

- the risk of arson and the risk of destruction of the warehouse and its stock were also foreseeable based on various guidance documents available to Sony prior to the fire
- Sony could have taken adequate security measures that probably would have deterred or delayed the attack on the warehouse and prevented the youths from gaining entry
- reasonable fire precautions, namely, the installation of sprinklers, probably would have suppressed the fire and significantly reduced any damage to the warehouse and its stock.

In summary, she concluded that the fire and resulting loss did not amount to circumstances beyond the reasonable control of Sony and therefore it was not open to Sony to rely on clause 14.1 as a defence.

In the light of this case the following points should be noted:

- foreseeability will be considered even where the clause does not expressly refer to this issue
- foreseeability will be assessed on the facts of each case
- if a contracting party could reasonably foresee the risk and did not take reasonable steps to prevent it then it will not be able to rely on a force majeure clause

4.2.2 Sample wording

Although a court will always consider issues of foreseeability, even in the absence of a specific clause addressing this issue, it is not uncommon for a specific clause to be inserted. I set out some examples below:

> *The Supplier cannot claim relief if the Force Majeure Event is one where a reasonable service provider should have foreseen and provided for the cause in question*

This clause contains a specific reference to foreseeability but also includes a reference to a 'reasonable service provider' which could allow room for further argument depending on the facts in each case.

> *A party cannot claim relief if the Force Majeure Event is attributable to that party's wilful act, neglect or failure to take reasonable precautions against the relevant Force Majeure Event*

This clause removes the caveat relating to 'reasonable service provider' and adds a specific reference to 'wilful act, neglect or failure'.

Clearly, a party seeking to be excused from its obligations would prefer the former clause as it allows more flexibility about what is required by way of prevention.

4.2.3 Covid-19

The key questions that arise here are:

(i) **whether the contracting party seeking to rely on the force majeure clause could have reasonably foreseen the emergence and extent of Covid-19 and/or the measures that would be taken by the government in response to it**

It could be argued that there have been similar epidemics before, for example Sars in 2003. Therefore, it was foreseeable that something like that may happen again and therefore the force majeure clause cannot be relied upon unless reasonable steps were taken to prevent the impact of Covid-19 and/or the governmental measures that were introduced.

However, I think that the better view is that the scale of Covid-19 and the scale of the government's response are, arguably, unprecedented. Certainly, there has not been such an outbreak in living memory and we have not seen such measures implemented since the end of the Second World War, Therefore, although some form of outbreak might have been foreseeable, an outbreak in the way that has happened and the government's response to it was arguably unforeseeable.

(ii) whether the inability to perform its obligations arose from the affected party's wilful act

As has been mentioned elsewhere in this book, the inability of a party to perform its obligations may be due to a voluntary act on its part rather than due to the disease or to an act of government. One example of this would be where a contracting party took a voluntary decision to close premises or suspend operations without being legally required to do so. If this was the case, the affected party would not be able to rely on the force majeure clause.

(iii) whether reasonable steps could have been taken to provide for the event

If we assume the event is the disease, then it could be argued that organisations could have taken reasonable steps in the following ways:

- introducing safe working practices, including social distancing and PPE, as soon as the disease was confirmed as being in the UK

- arranging alternative provision of goods and services from other organisations and countries that were less affected

If we assume the event is the government's measures, then it could be argued that organisations could have taken reasonable steps in the following ways:

- introducing new working practices allowing employees to continue working from home as far as possible

- lobbying the government to adopt measures that were more appropriate for specific sectors – e.g. airlines and accommodation

(iv) **reasonable service provider**

One final issue that could arise, depending on the wording of the clause, is whether there is a reference to 'reasonable service provider' and if so what this would mean for the steps that should have been taken by an affected party to prevent the impact of the force majeure event. This would require a consideration of available information and resources prior to the outbreak and is likely to vary considerably from case to case. However, it may be the case that the affected party's preparations were inadequate given its size and resources and therefore this could defeat an attempt to rely on a force majeure clause.

4.3 Mitigation

4.3.1 Guidance from case law

There is a general expectation in English law that any party seeking to rely on a force majeure clause will take steps to mitigate the effect of the force majeure event and resume performance as soon as possible. Where such a clause is found in a contract then it will often include a reference to the use of 'reasonable endeavours' and a good discussion of the relevant issues is found in the case of:

Seadrill Ghana Operations Limited v Tullow Ghana Limited[2]

The basic facts of this case were discussed in chapter 3 so will not be discussed again here. However, it is important to set out the relevant clauses before proceeding to analyse the judge's comments.

> *27.1 Neither COMPANY nor CONTRACTOR shall be responsible for any failure to fulfil any term or condition of the Contract if and to the extent that fulfilment has been delayed or temporarily prevented by an occurrence, as hereunder defined as FORCE MAJEURE, which has been notified in accordance with this Clause 27 and which is beyond the control and without the fault or negligence of the party affected and which, by the exercise of reasonable diligence, the said party is unable to prevent or provide against.* ***Both parties shall use their reasonable endeavours to mitigate, avoid, circumvent, or overcome the circumstances of FORCE MAJEURE."***
>
> *27.5 In the event of force majeure occurrence, the party that is or may be delayed in performing the Contract shall notify the other party without delay giving the full particulars thereof and* ***shall use all reasonable endeavours to remedy the situation without delay.***

In the light of these clauses the parties raised the following arguments:

- Seadrill argued that Tullow failed to exercise its reasonable endeavours to provide Seadrill with drilling instructions at wells in Jubilee or TEN which were not subject to the moratorium.

- Tullow responded by saying that it had exercised its reasonable endeavours, and was entitled to say that there was no business case for working on any of the wells suggested by Seadrill or that it was not in its commercial interests to do so.

2 [2018] EWHC 1640 (Comm) Teare J

The judge acknowledged that his ruling on causation rendered the issue of mitigation somewhat academic but proceeded to consider what the reasonable endeavours obligations required Tullow to do in terms of overcoming the force majeure event.

He made the following useful comments (on an obiter basis):

- the obligation required both parties to use reasonable endeavours to ensure that the force majeure event did not prevent them from performing their obligations under the contract or, if it did, to ensure that the effect of the force majeure was mitigated.

- as a matter of language "reasonable endeavours" was a phrase which enabled account to be taken of all matters which bore upon the question whether it was reasonable to expect a party to take certain steps to avoid or circumvent a force majeure.

- there was no reason to exclude the absence of a business case or Tullow's commercial interests from those matters which might be taken into account.

- however, the extent to which such matters might be taken into account and whether they were determinative would depend upon the contractual context in which the phrase was used.

He then proceeded to apply these principles to the facts at paragraphs 94-99:

'Tullow's obligation is to provide Seadrill with drilling instructions.

The contract area included TEN and Jubilee. Let it be assumed that Tullow was "delayed or temporarily prevented" from providing Seadrill with drilling instructions in TEN by reason of the moratorium.

In consequence Tullow's contractual duty was to exercise its reasonable endeavours to avoid or circumvent that prohibition by providing Seadrill with drilling instructions in Jubilee to the extent that was reasonable. If providing such instructions would be more expensive to Tullow than drilling in TEN or would be accompanied by a greater risk of a non-profitable outcome than drilling in TEN, such that it was not convenient to Tullow or in its interests to provide such instructions, Tullow would not be able to say (with regard to Jubilee) that fulfilment of a term or condition of the contract had been "delayed or temporarily prevented" by the moratorium. It would merely be more expensive or less attractive to Tullow.

That suggests that in the present context greater expense or a greater risk of an unprofitable outcome is not a matter which enables Tullow to say that it has exercised it reasonable endeavours.

Were it sufficient for Tullow to show that drilling in Jubilee was not in its commercial interest Tullow would be able to avoid its obligation to provide drilling instructions on the grounds of expense or expected lack of profit. That would be surprising in the present context. Tullow could not rely upon such matters to excuse non-performance before a force majeure and, in my judgment, it cannot do so after a force majeure.

The reason why in the present context, a force majeure clause, the mere fact that a step is contrary to a party's commercial interests is insufficient to show that it has exercised it reasonable endeavours is that in such context the party cannot ignore the commercial interests of the other party in the force majeure being avoided or circumvented.

That is apparent from the speech of Lord Devlin in Reardon Smith Line v Ministry of Agriculture, Fisheries and Food [1963] AC 691 at pp.729-730. Lord Devlin explained that when a contract provides that a party's obligation may be performed in a number of ways and he seeks to rely upon a force majeure or exceptions clause which bars one method of performance that party has a duty to perform his obligation in one of the other permitted ways

Thus, in my judgment, when drilling in TEN was prevented by the moratorium and Tullow was obliged to exercise its reasonable endeavours to avoid or circumvent the moratorium, Tullow was entitled to consider its own interests, and in particular, whether there was a business case for drilling at another well, but Tullow was also bound to consider the interests of Seadrill. It was not entitled to ignore the interest of Seadrill in receiving instructions for West Leo to drill at a well not affected by the moratorium.

Since Tullow is seeking to rely upon a force majeure to excuse it from non-performance of its obligations the burden lies upon Tullow to prove on the balance of probabilities that there was nothing that it could reasonably have done to avoid or circumvent the force majeure.

In conclusion, he ruled that Tullow had failed to exercise its reasonable endeavours to avoid or circumvent the force majeure.

In the light of this case the following points should be noted:

- when considering the issue of reasonable endeavours in the context of mitigation a party is entitled to consider its own commercial interests when deciding what steps, if any, to take

- however, in the context of a force majeure clause, it is important to consider the commercial interests of the other party as well

- where a party's obligations can be performed in a number of ways then if the force majeure bars the party from performance in one way it is expected to perform its obligations in one of the other permitted ways

4.3.2 Sample wording

Although a court will always consider issues of mitigation, even in the absence of a specific clause addressing this issue, it is not uncommon for a specific clause to be inserted as has been seen above. I set out some further examples below:

> *21.2 In the event that either party is delayed or prevented from or hindered in performing its obligations under this agreement by a Force Majeure Event such party shall:*
>
> *(a) use all reasonable endeavours to mitigate the effects of such delay or prevention on the performance of its obligations under this agreement; and*
>
> *(b) resume performance of its obligations as soon as reasonably possible after the removal of the cause of the delay or prevention*

The key features of this clause are as follows:

- the obligations only apply to the party seeking to be excused from its obligations
- there is a standard requirement to mitigate the effects of the delay or prevention
- resumption of performance will only take place once the cause of the delay or prevention has been removed

The last bullet point is the most controversial aspect of this clause. Some force majeure events may be over very quickly, for example a fire, while others may last for a considerable period of time, for example Covid-19. A party seeking to be excused from its obligations would be keen to insert such a clause while the other party would prefer it to be removed.

As soon as practicable following the affected party's notification, the parties shall consult with each other in good faith and use all reasonable endeavours to agree appropriate terms to mitigate the effects of the Force Majeure Event and to facilitate the continued performance of this agreement. Where the Supplier is the affected party, it shall take or procure the taking of all steps to overcome or minimise the consequences of the Force Majeure Event in accordance with best industry practice

The key features of this clause are as follows:

- the obligation to mitigate is a mutual one
- the parties are required to use all reasonable endeavours to mitigate and facilitate continued performance
- the Supplier is required to minimise the consequences in accordance with best industry practice

This clause is more customer friendly as it emphasises the need to facilitate continued performance rather than the importance of the force majeure event having come to an end. Furthermore, the burden on the supplier is a heavy one which is clearly greater than the obligation on the customer. The supplier would seek to amend this clause to include a reference to 'removal' of the force majeure and would also seek to water down the reference to 'best industry practice'.

4.3.3 Covid-19

In the context of Covid-19, a party seeking to rely either on the disease directly or on any subsequent acts of government would have to show that they had taken reasonable steps to mitigate the effect of the force majeure event. In practice this could mean the following type of actions:

- re-schedule or postpone an event until later in the year

- consider alternative ways of working so as to continue providing a basic service at least, for example a provider of training services that has traditionally only delivered face to face classroom-based training would be expected to implement e-learning as soon as reasonably practicable.

- ensure that social distancing and other appropriate health and safety considerations are implemented to allow employees to return to work as soon as possible

Of course, what is required by way of reasonable steps will be heavily driven by the facts in each case and the courts will not adopt a one size fits all approach. Furthermore, in the light of the Seadrill case a party seeking to rely on a force majeure clause must consider the other party's interests as well as its own.

4.4 Summary

In summary, the courts will always consider issues of prevention and mitigation when reviewing force majeure clauses and the parties may sometimes include their own clauses that refer expressly to such matters. Certainly, a customer would look to include specific requirements as discussed above which would make it more difficult for the supplier to rely on force majeure. The supplier would find it hard in practice to completely remove such provisions but would be keen to water them down in the ways suggested.

4.5 Practical steps

Customer

- insert a specific clause setting out references to foreseeability and prevention

- insert a specific clause requiring the supplier to mitigate the effects of the force majeure and to resume performance as soon as reasonably practicable

- add a reference requiring the supplier to use its reasonable endeavours to mitigate

Supplier

- ensure that reasonable precautions are taken to prevent the force majeure event arising

- limit your mitigation requirements as far as possible

- insert a reference to resumption of performance being dependent on the removal

- ensure that the mitigation requirements are mutual

CHAPTER FIVE
NOTIFICATION AND TERMINATION

5.1 Introduction

As has already been discussed, a force majeure clause operates to excuse one of the contracting parties from its obligations until such time as it is able to resume performance. Clearly, such a time-period will not be open-ended, and therefore it is commonplace for a force majeure clause to establish a period of time after which the contract can be terminated.

Calculating whether the time-period has elapsed or not then raises questions as to when the force majeure event began in the first place. One way that parties will try and resolve this is by adding a notification requirement into the clause so that the time-period only starts to run from the date of notification.

5.2 Notification

Notification clauses can cover two specific issues. The most common approach is to require the party relying on the force majeure clause to notify the other contracting party that the force majeure event has occurred. The other approach is to require the part relying on the force majeure clause to notify the other contracting party that the force majeure event has now concluded.

5.2.1 Notification of commencement

> *21.2 In the event that either party is delayed or prevented from or hindered in performing its obligations under this agreement by a Force Majeure Event such party shall:*

(a) give notice in writing of such delay or prevention to the other party as soon as reasonably possible stating the commencement date and extent of such delay or prevention and its estimated duration;

There are two main reasons why a customer would decide to include such a clause:

(i) Clarity about timing

There is a clear benefit to both parties to avoid arguments about fixing the date on which the failure to perform due to a force majeure event began.

(ii) Condition precedent

The addition of a notification provision effectively adds a condition precedent which must be satisfied by the affected party if it wants to rely on the clause. Furthermore, the customer could qualify the obligation further in terms of the level of detail that needed to be supplied. Given that the English courts interpret notice provisions strictly, this could mean that the supplier is prevented on relying on force majeure due to failing to comply with the necessary technicalities.

If a non-affected party does not insert such a clause then the affected party may fail to perform its obligations for several months and then suddenly announce that this was due to force majeure leading to a potentially costly and protracted dispute.

5.2.2 Notification of termination

21.6 The affected party shall notify the other party as soon as practicable after the Force Majeure Event ceases or no longer causes the affected party to be unable to comply with its obligations under this agreement. Following such notification, this agreement shall continue to be performed on the terms existing immediately prior to the occurrence of the Force Majeure Event unless agreed otherwise by the parties

Clauses requiring notification of termination of the force majeure event are less common but, nonetheless, can perform a useful function. The benefit of such a clause is also to ensure greater clarity about how long the impact of the force majeure event has lasted so as to avoid arguments about timing and entitlement to terminate.

5.3 Termination

There are two main issues that arise in respect of termination provisions as can be seen from the two sample clauses set out below:

If a Force Majeure Event continues for a period of more than six months from the date of its commencement, the non-affected shall be entitled to terminate this Agreement immediately on written notice to the other

Either party may, during the continuance of any Force Majeure Event, terminate this agreement by written notice to the other if a Force Majeure Event occurs that affects all or a substantial part of the services and which continues for more than 8 weeks

5.3.1 Period of time

Clearly the appropriate time-period will vary from one agreement to another. In particular, the time-period should aim for a balance between giving the affected party a realistic opportunity to resume performance and the need for the non-affected party to find an alternative solution if this is not possible.

5.3.2 Entitlement to terminate

As can be seen from the two clauses, it is possible to allow either party to terminate or to allow only the non-affected party to terminate. The danger with allowing either party to terminate is that the affected party could try and manipulate events so as to rely on the force majeure as a means to end a contract that was no longer profitable.[1] However, if there are clear notification requirements in place, this is less likely to occur and in any event the affected party must establish a causal link in order to rely upon the clause.

Another good reason why either party should be able to terminate is that otherwise the non-affected party could potentially refuse to terminate, and could continue to require the affected party to try and resume performance, even though this was not realistic.

On balance, the better view is that either party should be able to terminate the contract where performance cannot be resumed by the affected party within the specified time-period.

5.4 Covid-19

In terms of Covid-19 then careful attention should be paid to the following dates:[2]

- the date when Covid-19 was declared to be a pandemic by the WHO
- the date(s) when a certain percentage of the workforce were taken ill or required to shield in respect of Covid-19 so as to make performance of a party's obligations impossible

1 Seadrill v Tullow [supra]

2 Appendix 3 sets out a timeline of events

- the dates when specific restrictions were enacted by the UK government
- the date(s) on which employees were able to return to work even though Covid-19 remained classified as a pandemic
- the dates when certain restrictions were relaxed by the UK government
- the dates when certain restrictions were re-imposed by the UK government

As has been seen, there is a need to notify the other party that you are seeking to rely on a force majeure event as soon as reasonably practicable and therefore keeping a record of the aforementioned dates is important.

There may also be a further requirement to notify once the force majeure event has ceased or no longer prevents performance. Again, in terms of Covid-19 it is quite possible that the pandemic will continue but that it will be possible for employees to resume work either remotely or in person subject to satisfactory measures being put in place. All of this needs to be documented carefully.

Finally, a party wishing to terminate the contract due the stated time-period having expired will need to look carefully at the dates referred to above. Such a party will also need to check whether it is permitted to terminate under the clause or whether this right is reserved to the unaffected party only. In particular, care should be taken when relying on an act of Government as restrictions may be imposed, lifted and then re-instated. If restrictions are lifted, then arguably the force majeure event has ended but what will the effect be if the same restrictions are re-imposed? Will further notification be required, and will the time-period start again? These are questions that will, more than likely, be considered by the courts in years to come.

5.5 Summary

In summary, a notification provision is a sensible inclusion in any force majeure albeit the precise content will be the subject of some debate between the parties. In terms of termination provisions, a mutual right to terminate does open up the possibility of manipulation but the requirement of causation and also the insertion of a notification provision should be sufficient to prevent this from occurring too often in practice.

5.6 Practical steps

Customer

- insert a notification provision as a condition precedent
- insert a series of onerous requirements into the notice provision
- insert a short period of time into the termination provision
- try and reserve the sole right to terminate

Supplier

- amend the provisions of any notification clause so that they are not too onerous
- ensure that all necessary information is provided when giving notice
- consider whether a longer or shorter period of time should be inserted into the termination provision
- try and ensure a mutual right to terminate

CHAPTER SIX
TRADER TO CONSUMER CONTRACTS

6.1 Introduction

One of the most controversial aspects of the Covid-19 crisis has been the treatment of consumers by some traders, particularly in heavily affected sectors such as travel, accommodation and entertainment. In this chapter of the book, I will outline the general rules concerning unfair terms in consumer contracts, and will then outline the most recent guidance to traders that has been produced by the CMA.

6.2 Consumer Rights Act 2015 ('CRA')

There have been rules concerning unfair terms in consumer contracts since the 1990s and the most recent version of these rules in found in the CRA.[1]

6.2.1 Key principles:

The key principles are as follows:

- unfair terms are unenforceable against a consumer[2]

- a term is unfair if, contrary to the requirement of good faith, it causes a significant imbalance in the parties' rights and obligations under the contract to the detriment of the consumer[3]

---

1 http://www.legislation.gov.uk/ukpga/2015/15/contents

2 s62(1) CRA 2015

3 s62(4) CRA 2-15

- terms must be expressed in plain intelligible language and be legible[4]
- some clauses are exempted from the 'fairness' test[5]
- terms excluding or restricting a trader's liability in respect of breaches of ss9-17 and ss28-29 CRA 2015 are automatically unfair[6] (blacklist)

6.2.2 General guidance:

Schedule 2 of the CRA contains a list of 20 types of contract term that are likely to be considered unfair if used in a contract with a consumer (grey list). The full list can be accessed here:

http://www.legislation.gov.uk/ukpga/2015/15/schedule/2

The most relevant in the context of Covid-19 are:

2 *A term which has the object or effect of inappropriately excluding or limiting the legal rights of the consumer in relation to the trader or another party in the event of total or partial non-performance or inadequate performance by the trader of any of the contractual obligations, including the option of offsetting a debt owed to the trader against any claim which the consumer may have against the trader.*

7 *A term which has the object or effect of authorising the trader to dissolve the contract on a discretionary basis where the same facility is not granted to the consumer, or permitting the trader to retain the sums paid for services not yet supplied by the trader where it is the trader who dissolves the contract.*

---

4 s68(1)-(2) CRA 2015

5 s64(1)-(5) CRA 2015

6 s31 CRA 2016

This list is then supplemented by two documents produced by the CMA:

- Unfair contract terms guidance
- Annex A: historic examples of fair and unfair terms

These documents can be accessed here:

https://www.gov.uk/government/publications/unfair-contract-terms-cma37

These documents refer to a list of groupings numbered from 1-19 which supplement the list in schedule 2 of the CRA 2015. The most relevant in the context of Covid-19 are:

- Group 2(f) Exclusion of liability for delay
- Group 6(b) Supplier's right to cancel without refund
- Group 19 Use of plain and intelligible language

6.2.3 Specific Guidance

(i) 2(f) Exclusion of liability for delay (including force majeure)

The key points of the CMA's guidance in this area are as follows:

- goods should be delivered, and services performed on time
- the fact that delays can be caused by circumstances genuinely beyond the trader's control does not make it fair to exclude liability for all delays however caused

- clauses excluding liability for delay are more likely to be regarded as fair and thus to be enforceable where they are restricted in scope to delays unavoidably caused by factors beyond the trader's control

- such terms should not enable the trader to refuse redress where it is at fault, for example in not taking reasonable steps to prevent or minimise delay.

- where examples of such factors are stated, then, in order to be clearly fair, they should only be matters which are genuinely outside the trader's control, not situations such as shortage of stock, labour problems, etc, which can be the fault of the trader.

- the term 'force majeure' to describe events which are completely outside the trader's control is sometimes used in clauses of this kind. It is legal jargon and best avoided, and should never be used without clear explanation.

Examples of enforcement undertaken by the CMA in respect of this issue include the following:

Original term

> *The Company will make all reasonable endeavours to start and complete the works by the dates given but will not accept liability for delays.*

New term

> *The Company will do all that it reasonably can to meet the date given for delivery and/or installation. In the case of unforeseen circumstances, beyond the reasonable control of the company … the Company will contact the Customer and agree an alternative date.*

Original term

Whilst the company may quote a delivery period ... time for delivery shall not be of the essence of this contract and in the event of supplies or labour being adversely affected by strikes, lock outs or any other disruptions or contingencies beyond the company's control, the company shall not be held responsible for ... loss or liability incurred by the customer.

New term

We will make every effort to complete the work on time (or, if no date has been agreed, within a reasonable time from the date of your order) but we cannot be held responsible for delays due to weather or other circumstances beyond our control. In this case we will complete the work as soon as reasonably possible.

Original term

Crosville Wales Ltd ... will not be liable for any loss, hurt, damage, or inconvenience arising from the failure of its vehicles to start, to arrive at the time specified, or at all, due to circumstances beyond the Company's control, such as traffic delays, diversions, roadworks, mechanical breakdown ...

New term

... we cannot be held responsible for any inconvenience arising from failure to provide the advertised service because of factors which could reasonably be considered to be outside our control, such as adverse weather conditions or unpredictable delays caused by traffic congestion, road works, diversions or mechanical breakdowns which are unexpected and could not have been prevented by the proper execution of a reasonable preventative maintenance programme.

Original term

Where a time schedule has been agreed in writing with the customer the contractor will meet expenses reasonably incurred by the customer up to but not exceeding the cost of the removal or £150 whichever shall be the lesser amount. Nevertheless, the contractor shall not be liable for any such delay outside his control.

New term

If we do not keep to an agreed written time schedule and any delay is within our reasonable control we will pay your reasonable expenses which arise as a result of our not keeping to the agreed time schedule.

Original term

Dates specified for the commencement and completion of the work are estimates only and time shall not be of the essence of the contract.

New term

If we do not start or complete the work within 5 days of any date included in our estimate or quote you may nominate a date on which you want us to start the work or by which you want us to complete the work. If we have not started or completed the work by the date you have nominated you may cancel the agreement.

Original term

Times quoted are estimated times only and shall not be binding on the Company and the Company shall not accept any loss or liability whatsoever arising out of any failure to adhere to the times and dates quoted and nor shall any failure be deemed to be a breach of this contract.

New term

> *The Company will (subject to the company's duty to take reasonable care) install the units as efficiently and as quickly as is possible ...*

(ii) Para 6(b) Supplier's right to cancel without refund

The key points of the CMA's guidance in this area are as follows:

- cancellation clauses which allow the trader to cancel without acknowledging any right on the part of consumers to a refund of prepayments can be particularly open to abuse.

- as with cancellation rights generally, concern arises particularly where such a term could be used at the discretion of the trader.

- where a trader terminates a contract in response to a serious breach by the consumer, it may be entitled to retain all or some monies prepaid by the consumer, particularly by way of compensation for any loss directly caused by the breach.

- however, a term is likely to be subject to scrutiny if it makes a substantial prepayment non-refundable in all cases of termination on consumer default, regardless of whether any such loss has occurred.

- in most kinds of contract, a sudden and unexpected termination of the contract by the trader may cause inconvenience, and sometimes expense, for the consumer. Even in a 'continuing' contract, which by definition continues until one or other party cancels – for example a contract for cloud services – the trader should (with any other appropriate safeguards) normally give reasonable notice of termination.

- a right for the trader to cancel a contract without notice is less likely to raise concerns if its use is effectively restricted to situations in which there are 'serious grounds' for immediate termination. These might be circumstances in which there is a real risk of loss or harm to the trader or others if the contract continues for even a short period – for example, where there is a reasonable suspicion of fraud or other abuse.

- however, fairness is likely to require that clear indication is given of the nature of any 'serious grounds' for cancellation without notice. If the consumer will be unaware whether an immediate cancellation is or is not contractually justified, he or she is in no position to seek redress if it is not, and the term will in practice be open to abuse.

Three relevant enforcement examples are as follows:

Original term

> *Should ARTTS International be forced to close during term time on account of epidemic, national cause or any circumstances over which the staff have no control, fees cannot be returned ...*

New term

> *Should ARTTS International be forced to close during term time on account of an epidemic, national cause or any circumstances over which the Directors have no control, any pre-paid fees will be returned pro rata.*

Original term

> *No refund of fees will be given if pupils are suspended or expelled.*

New term

> *No refund of that term's fees will be given if pupils are suspended or expelled … If more than one term's fees have been prepaid, any surplus will be refunded.*

Original term

> *In the event of death we would expect the resident's bedroom to be cleared within 48 hours. In the event of death the home reserves the right to withhold [pre-paid fees] or charge for a period of 4 weeks.*

New term

> *In the event of death we would ask for the resident's bedroom to be cleared within three days. However if you are unable to do so, please inform the Matron/Manager straight away and arrangements can be made for us to clear the bedroom, and items can be stored at Penerley Lodge for seven days … In the event of death three days' monies will be due to the Home and after this period this contract will cease.*

(iii) Group 19 Plain intelligible language

As has been noted earlier in this chapter, there is a general requirement in the CRA that terms should be expressed using 'plain and intelligible language'[7]. This requirement is also found in group 19 of the CMA's groupings. One relevant enforcement example in respect of force majeure is as follows:

Original term

> *Force Majeure. Time shall not be of the essence of the Contract and the Company shall not be liable for any delay in installation in the event of any strike, lock out, trade dispute, accident, fire, flood or any*

7 s68(2) CRA 2015

natural disaster or act of God or any contingency whatsoever beyond the reasonable control of the Company affecting the supply or installation of the Contract overleaf. Such suspension or cancellation shall not constitute a breach of Contract by the Company, nor will the purchaser be liable to claim for any loss or damage howsoever arising as a result of these circumstances.

New term

The Company will manufacture and install the items within a reasonable time.

(iv) Summary

As can be seen, the CMA has always been concerned about traders excluding liability for delay, retaining unequal cancellation rights and hiding behind legal jargon. When applied to Covid-19, it is hardly surprising that the CMA does not typically see force majeure as a valid reason for traders to refuse to provide refunds in respect of delay or non-performance of their obligations and/or cancellation of contracts.

6.3 CMA Covid-19 Guidance

The CMA established a Covid-19 task force on 20th March 2020 and published the following document on 30th April 2020:

Covid-19 – pandemic, consumer contracts, cancellation and refunds – 30th April 2020

https://www.gov.uk/government/publications/cma-to-investigate-concerns-about-cancellation-policies-during-the-coronavirus-covid-19-pandemic/the-coronavirus-covid-19-pandemic-consumer-contracts-cancellation-and-refunds

This document draws heavily on the existing law as outlined above but places particular emphasis on specific Covid-19 related matters. I set out a series of relevant extracts below:

> ***Refunds***
>
> *Where a contract is not performed as agreed, the CMA considers that consumer protection law will generally allow consumers to obtain a refund.*
>
> *In particular, for most consumer contracts the CMA would expect a consumer to be offered a full refund where:*
>
> - *a business has cancelled a contract without providing any of the promised goods or services;*
> - *no service is provided by a business, for example because this is prevented by Government public health measures;*
> - *a consumer cancels, or is prevented from receiving any services, because Government public health measures mean they are not allowed to use the services.*
>
> ***Exceptions***
>
> *Sometimes, a consumer will already have received some of the services they have paid for in advance. In those cases, the CMA considers that the consumer would normally be entitled to at least a refund for the services that are not provided. However, where they have already received something of value, consumers should generally be expected to pay for it and they will not usually be entitled to get all their money back.*
>
> *In some cases, where Government public health measures prevent a business from providing a service or the consumer from receiving it,*

the business may be able to deduct a contribution to the costs it has already incurred in relation to the specific contract in question (where it cannot recover them elsewhere). In the CMA's view, these cases are likely to be relatively rare, however, and the costs that may be deducted from refunds will usually be limited.

Ongoing contracts

Where a consumer receives regular services in exchange for a regular payment as part of an ongoing contract, the CMA considers that consumer protection law:

- *will normally require the consumer to be offered a refund for any services they have already paid for but that are not provided by the business or which the consumer is not allowed to use because of Government public health measures (this may be a partial refund of the total amount the consumer has paid, to reflect the value of the services already provided);*
- *will normally allow the consumer to withhold payment for services that are not provided by the business or which the consumer is not allowed to use because of Government public health measures;*
- *may allow a business to require payment of a small contribution to its costs until the provision of the service is resumed, but only where the contract terms set this out clearly and fairly.*

Non-refundable payments and fees

In the CMA's view, the above rights to a refund will usually apply even where the consumer has paid what the business says is a non-refundable deposit or advance payment.

The CMA also considers that businesses should not charge an admin fee (or equivalent) for processing refunds in the above circumstances.

Credits and re-booking

Consumers can normally be offered credits, vouchers, re-booking or re-scheduling as an alternative to a refund, but they should not be misled or pressured into doing so, and a refund should still be an option that is just as clearly and easily available. Any restrictions that apply to credits, vouchers, re-booking or re-scheduling, such as the period in which credits must be used or services re-booked, must also be fair and made clear to consumers.

Timing

The CMA accepts that, in the circumstances, it may take businesses longer than normal to process refunds. The timeframes for providing refunds should be made clear to consumers and refunds should still be given within a reasonable time (and, where there are statutory deadlines for payment – like those which apply to package holidays – businesses should take those into account).

Future contracts

Some contracts may require consumers to pay now for services they will receive in the future, after the current disruption has lifted. A business should not seek payments for a service it knows it will be unable to provide. Where the business reasonably expects to provide the service as agreed, the CMA's view is that, in general, the business can require consumers to carry on making these payments for the time being. That could be the case, for example, for some services due to be provided later in the year. Consumers' rights to refunds will depend on whether the services can be provided when the time comes.

Cancellation by consumers for other reasons

> *If a consumer cancels a contract because they no longer want the service, even though the service can still be provided as agreed, the consumer will be entitled to a refund in line with the applicable terms and conditions (on the assumption those terms are fair).*

During the period 10th March 2020 to 17th May 2020 the CMA had been contacted more than 60,000 times about coronavirus related issues.[8] At the time of writing the CMA has now opened formal investigations into the following sectors:

- Weddings and private events
- Holiday accommodation
- Package holidays
- Nurseries and childcare providers

6.4 Summary

In summary, the default position in respect of a trader to consumer contract affected by Covid-19 is that the consumer should be offered a full refund in the vast majority of cases. Failure to do so may lead to enforcement action as well as considerable damage to the trader's reputation.

8 Update on CMA Covid-19 Taskforce – 21st May 2020
https://www.gov.uk/government/news/update-on-cma-covid-19-taskforce

6.5 Practical steps

- review any trader to consumer contracts to ensure that they are compliant with the requirements of the CRA
- ensure that if you cancel a consumer contract you offer a refund as well as other potential remedies

- if you are intending to withhold any sums on account of costs and expenses, ensure that this is clearly stated in the contract and point this out to the consumer

PART B

ALTERNATIVES TO FORCE MAJEURE

This section of the book sets out a series of approaches that may be adopted, in a business to business context, where force majeure is not available, or where the parties decide to adopt a more conciliatory approach. Each chapter focusses on a different issue and, having outlined the key content, concludes with a series of practical steps to be considered by the reader.

The chapters are as follows:

7. Frustration
8. Other Contract Considerations
9. Commercial Alternatives

CHAPTER SEVEN
FRUSTRATION

7.1 Introduction

Frustration is a well-established common law doctrine that operates to bring a contract to an end because of a supervening event. Its primary purpose has been defined in the following terms:

> *'The doctrine of frustration was evolved to mitigate the rigour of the common law's insistence on literal performance of absolute promises. The object of the doctrine was to give effect to the demands of justice, to achieve a just and equitable result, to do what is reasonable and fair, as an expedient to escape from injustice where such would result from enforcement of a contract in its literal terms after a significant change in circumstances'.*[1]

However, due to this draconian effect, its application is by no means guaranteed and, in this chapter, I summarise the key issues that need to be borne in mind.

7.2 Relationship with force majeure

The insertion of a force majeure clause into a contract means that the doctrine of frustration is less likely to apply. This is particularly the case where the contracting parties have made express provision for an event that occurs (for example 'pandemic' or 'act of government'). Ultimately, the broader the definition of force majeure, the narrower the scope for frustration.

---

1 J Lauritzen AS v Wijsmuller BV, The Super Servant Two [1989] EWCA Civ 6 Bingham LJ

However, even if a contract contains a force majeure clause, the courts may construe the clause as not covering a specific event. Some guidance on this issue may be obtained from the following judicial statement:

> *'The theory of dissolution of a contract by the frustration of its commercial object rests on an implication, which arises from the presumed common intention of the parties. "Where the contract makes provision" (that is, full and complete provision, so intended) "for a given contingency it is not for the Court to import into the contract some other and different provision for the same contingency called by a different name". This is a matter of construction according to the usual rule.'*[2]

The key phrase here is 'full and complete provision'. Where the force majeure clause is drafted narrowly it is possible to argue that it has not made full and complete provision for what has occurred and therefore the doctrine of frustration may still be relevant.

7.3 Definition

The following tests for frustration have been provided by the courts (key phrases highlighted):

> *"...frustration occurs whenever the law recognises that without default of either party a contractual obligation has become* ***incapable of being performed*** *because the circumstances in which performance is called for would render it a thing* ***radically different*** *from that which was undertaken by the contract. Non haec in foedera veni. It was not this that I promised to do."*[3]

> *"Frustration of a contract takes place where there* ***supervenes an event*** *(without default of either party and for which the contract*

---

2 Bank Line Ltd v Arthur Capel & Co [1919] AC 435

3 Davis Contractors Ltd v. Fareham UDC, Lord Radcliffe [1956] 1 AC 696 at 729.

makes no sufficient provision) which ***so significantly changes the nature*** *(not merely the expense or onerousness) of the outstanding contractual rights and/or obligations* ***from what the parties could reasonably have contemplated*** *at the time of its execution that it would be unjust to hold them to the literal sense of its stipulations in the new circumstances: in such case, the law declares both parties to be discharged from further performance."*[4]

The key points to note from these two judicial statements are as follows:

- some form of supervening event must occur (not attributable to either party and not reasonably contemplated by them)

- which means that the circumstances in which performance would now take place would significantly change the nature of the outstanding contractual rights so as to render what was due to be delivered radically different from what was originally envisaged

- in such circumstances the only just outcome would be to release the parties from their obligations and bring the contract to an end

In terms of Covid-19, either the disease itself or an act of government could potentially constitute such a supervening event but whether either of these events caused sufficient change leading to radically different results would need to be considered on a case by case basis.

4 National Carriers Ltd v. Panalpina (Northern) Ltd, Lord Simon [1981] AC 675

7.4 Key considerations

When considering whether an event gives rise to frustration of a contract, the courts apply what is termed a multi-factorial approach which requires a review of at least the following factors:[5]

- *the terms of the contract itself,*
- *its matrix or context,*
- *the parties' knowledge, expectations, assumptions and contemplations, in particular as to risk, as at the time of contract, at any rate so far as these can be ascribed mutually and objectively,*
- *and then the nature of the supervening event, and*
- *the parties' reasonable and objectively ascertainable calculations as to the possibilities of future performance in the new circumstances.*

In terms of Covid-19, the key questions to be considered by the court would be as follows:

- did the contract contain a force majeure clause and if so did it make 'full and complete provision' for either the disease or an act of government?
- what were the key obligations being performed under the contract and what was the likely impact of the disease or an act of government upon these obligations?
- how likely was it that such events could occur?

---

5 Edwinton Commercial Corp v Tsavliris Russ (Worldwide Salvage & Towage) Ltd (The Sea Angel) [2007] 2 Lloyd's Rep 517 Rix LJ – para 111

- was the supervening event relied upon the disease itself or the resulting actions of the government?
- how realistic was it for the parties to continue to perform their obligations during the duration of the supervening event or following its conclusion?

7.5 Examples from case law

There are relatively few reported cases on the topic of frustration and this is perhaps a reflection of the increased use of force majeure clauses by contracting parties. However, there are some cases that can provide insight and I set out a brief summary of these below.

7.5.1 Cancellation of an expected event

There a series of cases relating to the postponement of the coronation procession of Kind Edward VII. The cancellation of this expected event was held to constitute frustrating event in certain cases.[6]

In terms of Covid-19, cancellation of sporting and similar events could constitute a frustrating event in respect of related contracts such as provision of hospitality and catering which could no longer go ahead as the main event had been cancelled.

7.5.2 Act of government

There are two cases where an act of government has been held to be a frustrating event:

6 Krell v Henry [1903] 2 KB 740

(i) Change in the law – supervening illegality[7]

In June 1914 the Metropolitan Water Board engaged a firm of contractors to construct a reservoir over a six-year period. The work began but in February 1916 the Minister of Munitions ordered the construction work to cease and requisitioned part of the area under construction. The contractors argued that the purpose of the contract was frustrated due to supervening illegality.

The House of Lords held that:

> *'the interruption was of such a character and duration as fundamentally to change the conditions of the contract, and could not have been in the contemplation of the parties to the contract when it was made. Accordingly the contract had ceased to be operative.'*

In terms of Covid-19, if specific regulations enacted by the government required a contracting party to close its business for a period of time then this could constitute a frustrating event.

(ii) Government requisition of a contract's subject matter[8]

In this case a ship was requisitioned by the British government and the House of Lords held that this did constitute a frustrating event which brought the ship's charter to an end.

In terms of Covid-19, the Government could decide to requisition buildings, venues or equipment for purposes related to providing testing venues, additional hospitals or manufacture of ventilators. If this happened it could constitute a frustrating event in respect of existing contracts that the affected businesses are no longer able to perform as a result of the government's actions.

---

7 Metropolitan Water Board v Dick, Kerr & Co Ltd [1918] AC 119

8 Bank Line Ltd v Arthur Capel & Co [1918] UKHL 1

At present this is fairly unlikely, as such actions have typically been taken with the consent of the businesses affected. For example, businesses that are not operating have been willing to allow available space to be used for testing purposes on the understanding that they have a right to terminate the arrangement in due course.

7.5.3 Abnormal delay[9]

This case concerned a claimant with fluctuating capacity to conduct legal proceedings. At a time when she had capacity, she retained a firm of solicitors under a conditional fee agreement ("CFA"). The defendants argued that the CFA terminated automatically by reason of frustration when the claimant subsequently lost capacity. Therefore, the CFA did not govern the continued conduct of the proceedings by a receiver/deputy appointed by the Court of Protection to act on her behalf.

Both the High Court and the Court of Appeal rejected this argument and held that the CFA was not frustrated.

However, one of the issues raised in this case was that of frustration arising from delay and this was commented on in the High Court decision at paragraph 40:

> *'... even if any delay caused by supervening incapacity was not within the scope of the contractual terms, it is clear that mere delay does not frustrate a contract. It would only amount to a frustrating event if the delay is "abnormal, in its cause, its effect or its expected duration, so that it falls outside what the parties could reasonably contemplate at the time of contracting": see Chitty on Contracts 31st ed. para 23-035. Given that a claimant may regain capacity or otherwise have a deputy in place in short order, the delay arising from*

9 Blankley v Central Manchester [2014] EWHC 168 (QB) Phillips J, [2015] EWCA Civ 18 Richards LJ

supervening incapacity would not seem to be of sufficient expected duration to regard the retainer as having been frustrated.'

In terms of Covid-19, it is quite probable that performance of contractual obligations may be delayed for some time. However, the key issue would be at what point such a delay became abnormal. To a large extent this would be determined by the duration of the pandemic and also any relevant restrictions on businesses operating.

7.5.4 Summary

In summary, these cases suggest that there is at least some possibility of relying on frustration in the context of Covid-19. However, the most recent case considered by the courts, in the context of Brexit demonstrates, that this is by no means a foregone conclusion.

Canary Wharf (BP4) T1 Limited v European Medicines Agency [2019] EWHC 335 (Ch)

The parties entered into a 25-year lease in October 2014 in respect of office premises at Canary Wharf. The lease did not contain a break clause but did allow sub-letting and assignment.

In 2017 the UK Government formally invoked Article 50 thereby beginning the process of the UK's withdrawal from the EU. In August 2017 the EMA decided to re-locate its headquarters to Amsterdam and sent the following letter to Canary Wharf (BP4) its landlord:

'Having considered the position under English law, we have decided to inform you that if and when Brexit occurs, we will be treating that event as frustration of the Lease'

The landlord then sought a declaration from the High Court that Brexit did not constitute a frustrating event.

Submissions of EMA

EMA put forward two reasons why the contract should be viewed as being frustrated:

(i) Frustration of common purpose

The common purpose of the lease was to provide a permanent headquarters for EMA until 2039. However, EMA was no longer able to occupy the premises or make profitable use of them due to EU law and therefore the common purpose had been frustrated.

(ii) Supervening illegality

The withdrawal of the UK from the EU changed the legal landscape within which EMA operated. This meant that actions on the part of EMA (i.e. performing their obligations under the lease) which had previously been lawful were now unlawful.

High Court Decision

The High Court outlined the key principles discussed earlier in this chapter and then ruled that the lease would not be frustrated by Brexit, even in the case of a no-deal Brexit, for the following reasons:

(i) Frustration of common purpose

- there was no additional common purpose over and above the construction of the lease
- the supervening event was EMA's involuntary departure from the premises as a result of circumstances beyond its reasonable control
- sub-letting / assignment was permitted

- the UK's departure from the EU was not expressly provided for but the re-location of the EMA away from the premises was provided for

(ii) Supervening illegality

- in the event of Brexit the EMA continued to have the capacity to deal with the property and pay the rent

- this would also be the case in the event of a no-deal Brexit

In summary, the High Court ruled that the impact of Brexit did not make performance 'radically different' from what was originally intended

In the light of this case the following points should be noted:

- the rules on frustration do apply to commercial leases

- it will be difficult to establish that Brexit will frustrate a contract but it is important to note that each case will be highly fact sensitive

- if difficulties are envisaged in the light of Brexit the better course of action would be to begin discussing contract amendments now to take these matters into account

This case serves to highlight that just because something has happened to make the operation of a contract more difficult does not necessarily mean that the contract is frustrated. This is an important point to remember when considering the true impact of Covid-19.

7.6 Limits

The following judicial statement provides an insight into the courts' thinking on this issue:

> *Since the effect of frustration is to kill the contract and discharge the parties from further liability under it, the doctrine must not be lightly invoked and must be kept within very narrow limits.*[10]

The same case also established two specific limits that apply in respect of frustration:

7.6.1 Act or election

The essence of frustration is that it should not be due to the act or election of the party seeking to rely on it. In terms of Covid-19, the key questions are as follows:

- did the party relying on frustration take voluntary action of its own in anticipation of Covid-19?; or
- were its actions as a result of the disease occurring among employees or specific restrictions introduced by the government?

Clearly, voluntary actions are unlikely to constitute a frustrating event.

7.6.2 Blame or fault

A frustrating event must take place without blame or fault on the side of the party seeking to rely on it. In terms of Covid-19, the key questions are as follows:

10 J Lauritzen AS [supra]

- did the party relying on frustration make the situation worse by failing to comply with restrictions or by failing take sensible precautions?; or

- did it do everything reasonably possible and only failed to perform its obligations due to the disease occurring among its employees or due to the specific restrictions imposed by the government

If the contracting party made the situation worse by its actions, then those actions are unlikely to constitute a frustrating event.

7.7 Foreseeability

In addition to these limits, the courts will also consider the issue of foreseeability:

> *'In a sense, most events are to a greater or lesser degree foreseeable. That does not mean that they cannot lead to frustration. Even events which are not merely foreseen but made the subject of express contractual provision may lead to frustration: as occurs when an event such as a strike, or a restraint of princes, lasts for so long as to go beyond the risk assumed under the contract and to render performance radically different from that contracted for. However, as Treitel shows through his analysis of the cases, and as Chitty summarises, the less that an event, in its type and its impact, is foreseeable, the more likely it is to be a factor which, depending on other factors in the case, may lead on to frustration.'* [11]

The general rule is that if the event was indeed foreseeable, and was foreseen, by the parties then frustration will not apply. However, the less likely that an event is foreseeable the more likely it may lead to frustration.

---

11 The Sea Angel [supra] (paragraph 127)

In terms of Covid-19, as discussed earlier in this book in the context of force majeure, my view is that the occurrence of some sort of pandemic was foreseeable but the extent of the spread of Covid-19 was less foreseeable and the response by governments even less so. Assuming that all of the other criteria are satisfied I think that foreseeability is unlikely to pose too much of a barrier to relying on frustration.

7.8 Effect of frustration

The effect of frustration can be summed up by the following judicial statement:[12]

> *'Frustration brings the contract to an end forthwith, without more and automatically. It does not require an act by the parties to the contract.'*

Of course, frustration is likely to lead to further arguments between the parties as to the recoverability of payments made in anticipation of work and also the impact on sums that were payable but have not yet been paid. This issue is addressed to some extent in the following legislation:

Law Reform (Frustrated Contracts) Act 1943 ('LRFCA')

This legislation followed the decision in the case of **Fibrosa SA v Fairbairn Lawson Combe Barber Ltd**[13] and contains the following key provisions:

12 J Lauritzen AS [supra]

13 [1943] AC 32

7.8.1 Sums paid or payable[14]

All sums paid or payable to any party in pursuance of the contract before the time when the parties were so discharged (in this Act referred to as "the time of discharge") shall, in the case of sums so paid, be recoverable from him as money received by him for the use of the party by whom the sums were paid, and, in the case of sums so payable, cease to be so payable:

Provided that, if the party to whom the sums were so paid or payable incurred expenses before the time of discharge in, or for the purpose of, the performance of the contract, the court may, if it considers it just to do so having regard to all the circumstances of the case, allow him to retain or, as the case may be, recover the whole or any part of the sums so paid or payable, not being an amount in excess of the expenses so incurred.

7.8.2 Valuable benefit[15]

Where any party to the contract has, by reason of anything done by any other party thereto in, or for the purpose of, the performance of the contract, obtained a valuable benefit (other than a payment of money to which the last foregoing subsection applies) before the time of discharge, there shall be recoverable from him by the said other party such sum (if any), not exceeding the value of the said benefit to the party obtaining it, as the court considers just, having regard to all the circumstances of the case and, in particular,—

(a) the amount of any expenses incurred before the time of discharge by the benefited party in, or for the purpose of, the performance of the contract, including any sums paid or payable by him to any other party in pursuance of the contract and retained or recoverable by that party under the last foregoing subsection, and

14 s1(2) Law Reform (Frustrated Contracts) Act 1943

15 s1(3) LRFCA 1943

(b) the effect, in relation to the said benefit, of the circumstances giving rise to the frustration of the contract.

7.8.3 Exceptions[16]

This Act shall not apply—

(a) to any charterparty, except a time charterparty or a charterparty by way of demise, or to any contract (other than a charterparty) for the carriage of goods by sea; or

(b) to any contract of insurance, save as is provided by subsection (5) of the foregoing section; or

(c) to any contract to which section 7 of the Sale of Goods Act 1979 (which avoids contracts for the sale of specific goods which perish before the risk has passed to the buyer) applies, or to any other contract for the sale, or for the sale and delivery, of specific goods, where the contract is frustrated by reason of the fact that the goods have perished.

Although these provisions are undoubtedly helpful, the reality is that the courts will still be required to consider each case on its merits.

7.9 Summary:

In summary, the application of frustration to a particular scenario related to Covid-19 or otherwise will depend largely on the presence or absence of a force majeure clause in the contract that is affected. However, as has been seen, even where a force majeure clause is present it is still possible to argue that it does not make 'full and complete provision' for the event in question.

16 s2(5) LRFCA 1943

Nevertheless, in the context of Covid-19 it is certainly worth arguing frustration either in its own right or as an alternative to force majeure albeit noting that the courts will only be prepared to invoke this doctrine within the strict limits outlined above.

7.10 Practical steps

A party seeking to rely on frustration should consider the following steps:

- argue that any force majeure clause does not make 'full and complete provision' for the event in question
- consider carefully the issues set out as part of the multi-factorial approach
- argue that the event does significantly change the nature of the contractual obligations so that what is now possible is radically different from what was originally intended
- argue that the event is not due to its act or election
- argue that it was not at fault in respect of the event
- argue that the event was not reasonably foreseeable

A party opposing frustration should consider the following steps:

- argue that the contract's force majeure clause does make 'full and complete provision' for the event in question
- consider carefully the issues set out as part of the multi-factorial approach

- argue that the event does not significantly change the nature of the contractual obligations so that what is now possible is radically different from what was originally intended
- argue that the event is due to the act or election of the party seeking to rely on it
- argue that the party seeking to rely on frustration was at fault in respect of the event
- argue that the event was reasonably foreseeable

CHAPTER EIGHT
OTHER CONTRACT CONSIDERATIONS

8. Other Contract Considerations

8.1 Introduction

Alongside considerations of force majeure and frustration, there are two other issues that need to be borne in mind. First, there may be other specific clauses that can be relied upon either to terminate the contract or to argue that failure to perform obligations is either acceptable or unacceptable. Furthermore, on the 7th May 2020, the government published a guidance note on 'fair behaviour' in the context of contracts and Covid-19. Each of these issues will now be considered in turn.

8.2 Specific contract clauses

There are two specific contract clauses that should be considered.

8.2.1 Termination clauses

Typically, contracts will contain a termination clause which may allow either party to terminate subject to a period of notice. If one of the contracting parties is of the opinion that the impact of Covid-19 is so severe that the contract should not continue, then the first option is to consider whether the contract can be brought to an end using such a clause. The benefit of this is that complex arguments concerning force majeure and frustration can be avoided and this would lead to a non-contentious solution.

However, break clauses may be subject to certain specific conditions concerning when they can be triggered and by whom as well as setting out requirements as to the form and content of the notice. Consequently, the ability to rely on such a clause is by no means guaranteed.

8.2.2 Good faith clauses

In recent years it has become increasingly common to insert express good faith clauses into contracts governed by English law. Good faith is defined in English law as:[1]

> *'An obligation to act honestly and with fidelity to the bargain; an obligation not to act dishonestly and not to act to undermine the bargain entered or the substance of the contractual benefit bargained for; and an obligation to act reasonably and with fair dealing having regard to the interests of the parties (which will, inevitably, at times conflict) and to the provisions, aims and purposes of the contract, objectively ascertained.'*

In the context of Covid-19, or a similar event, certain actions taken under a contract, including termination, either directly or indirectly linked to that event could constitute a breach of such an obligation.

Often this will depend on the way in which the good faith obligation has been drafted as this will then determine whether the good faith obligation is confined to a particular clause or applies more widely to all of the provisions in the contract. Guidance as to how the wording found in such clauses will be interpreted may be obtained from two recent cases:

1 Al Nehayan v Kent [2018] EWHC 333 (Comm) Leggatt LJ

(i) Narrow application[2]

*'3.5 The Trust and the Contractor will co-operate with each other in **good faith** and will take all reasonable action as is necessary for the efficient transmission of information and instructions and to enable the Trust or, as the case may be, any Beneficiary to derive the full benefit of the Contract. At all times in the performance of the Services, the Contractor will co-operate fully with any other contractors appointed by the Trust or any Beneficiary in connection with other services at the Location.'*

In this case the Court of Appeal ruled that the good faith obligation in clause 3.5 was confined only to the obligations referred to in the clause and did not apply more broadly. In such a case it is unlikely that any action taken in respect of Covid-19 would constitute a breach of this clause unless it was in respect of the matters specifically mentioned therein.

(ii) Broad application[3]

'3.1 HCML shall act in good faith towards TPN at all times.'

In this case the High Court ruled that the good faith obligation in clause 3.1 applied to entirety of the parties' obligations under the contract. Consequently, in this case, it is far more likely that action taken in the light of Covid-19 could constitute a breach of this clause.

---

2 Mid Essex Hospital Services NHS Trust v Compass Group UK and Ireland Ltd (t/a Medirest) [2013] EWCA Civ 200 (15 March 2013)

3 Health & Case Management Limited v The Physiotherapy Network [2018] EWHC 869 (QB) Nicklin J

8.3 Implied obligations of good faith

Another good faith related issue which may arise in the context of Covid-19 and other similar events is that of implied obligations of good faith. The key considerations relating to this issue were set out in the judgment of Leggatt J (as he then was) in the leading authority of Yam Seng[4].

- it is a well-established principle of English contract law that there is no duty of good faith that it is automatically implied into all contracts

- however, such a duty could be implied, using the standard tests for implied terms, in respect of certain types of contracts, namely
    - necessary for business efficacy
    - so obvious it goes without saying

- this would particularly be the case in respect of so called 'relational contracts'

- relational contracts are defined as being contracts that:

  'may require a high degree of communication, cooperation and predictable performance based on mutual trust and confidence and involve expectations of loyalty which are not legislated for in the express terms of the contract but are implicit in the parties' understanding and necessary to give business efficacy to the arrangements'

- examples of such contracts can include (but are not limited to):

---

4 Yam Seng PTE Ltd v International Trade Corporation Ltd [2013] EWHC 111 (QB) (01 February 2013)

- *'some joint venture agreements*
- *franchise agreements; and*
- *long term distributorship agreements.'*

These principles have now been applied in a number of High Court cases. Some confusion appeared to arise in the case Bates v Post Office (3)[5] where Fraser J held that there was an implied obligation of good faith but placed rather more emphasis on whether the contract was relational rather than on applying the two implied terms tests referred to above.

This approach was criticised in the more recent case of UTB v Sheffield United[6] where the judge stated that the relevant question to be asked was:

> *'whether a reasonable person reading the ISA at the time that it was made, with knowledge of the circumstances in which it is entered into (though not the negotiations of the parties or their drafts and preparatory documents) and the other agreements made as part of the same transaction, would consider that it was* ***obvious*** *that UTB had to act in good faith in all its dealings with SUL, and vice versa, or whether such an obligation is* ***necessary to give coherent business effect*** *to the ISA.'*

In summary, even in the absence of express good faith provisions, it is possible that actions taken in respect of Covid-19 may still be in breach of an implied obligation of good faith depending on the nature of the contract and the context in which it was entered into.

5 [2019] EWHC 606 (QB) Fraser J

6 [2019] EWHC 2322 (Ch) Fancourt J

8.4 Government guidance

In response to the Covid-19 crisis, the Government published the following document on 7th May 2020:

Guidance on responsible contractual behaviour in the performance and enforcement of contracts impacted by the Covid-19 emergency

This document can be accessed here:

https://www.gov.uk/government/publications/guidance-on-responsible-contractual-behaviour-in-the-performance-and-enforcement-of-contracts-impacted-by-the-covid-19-emergency

I set out some relevant extracts below:

> ***Responsible and fair contractual behaviour***
>
> *14. Responsible and fair behaviour is strongly encouraged in performing and enforcing contracts where there has been a material impact from Covid-19. This includes being reasonable and proportionate in responding to performance issues and enforcing contracts (including dealing with any disputes), acting in a spirit of cooperation and aiming to achieve practical, just and equitable contractual outcomes having regard to the impact on the other party (or parties), the availability of financial resources, the protection of public health and the national interest.*
>
> *15. In particular, responsible and fair behaviour is strongly encouraged in relation to the following:*
>
> *(a) requesting, and giving, relief for impaired performance, including in respect of the time for delivery and completion, the nature and scope of goods, works and services, the making of payments and the operation of payment and performance mechanisms;*

(b) requesting, and allowing, extensions of time, substitute or alternative performance and compensation, including compensation for increased cost or additional performance;

(c) making, and responding to, force majeure, frustration, change in law, relief event, delay event, compensation event and excusing cause claims;

(d) requesting, and making, payment under the contract;

(e) making, and responding to, claims for damages, including under liquidated damages provisions;

(f) returning deposits or part payments;

(g) exercising remedies in respect of impaired performance, including enforcement of security, forfeiture or repossession of property, calling of bonds or guarantees or the initiation or continuation of insolvency or winding up (or equivalent) proceedings;

(h) claiming breach of contract and enforcing events of default and termination provisions (including termination rights arising by reason of the insolvency or potential insolvency of a party);

(i) making, and responding to, requests for information and data under the contract;

(j) giving notices, keeping records and providing reports under the contract (recognising that the need to keep records of contractual behaviours and decisions, including the behaviours referred to in this guidance, is important);

(k) making, and responding to, requests for contract changes and variations;

(l) making, and responding to, requests for consents (including funder consents);

(m) commencing, and continuing, formal dispute resolution procedures, including proceedings in court;

(n) requesting, and responding to, requests for mediation or other alternative or fast-track dispute resolution; and

(o) enforcing judgments.

16. The responsible and fair behaviour described in paragraphs 14 and 15 should continue to apply in circumstances where the relevant contract is materially impacted by Covid-19, so that fair and equitable outcomes can be achieved in contractual arrangements and the objectives described in paragraph 13 can be met.

17. It is recognised in particular that disputes, especially a "plethora of disputes", can be destructive to good contractual outcomes and the effective operation of markets. Further to paragraphs 15(m) and 15(n), the Government would strongly encourage parties to seek to resolve any emerging contractual issues responsibly – through negotiation, mediation or other alternative or fast-track dispute resolution – before these escalate into formal intractable disputes. For example, the Construction Industry Council and the Royal Institution of Chartered Surveyors (RICS) have developed the Low Value Disputes Model Adjudication Procedure. RICS also developed the Conflict Avoidance Pledge (and an associated Conflict Avoidance Procedure) for early resolution of disputes and is expected to launch a fast-track (15-day) adjudication service which will have capped fees.

In practice this document has no binding force. However, in the light of previous discussions in this chapter about good faith obligations, failure to comply with the spirit of this document could be raised as a breach of good faith. Therefore, my recommendation would be to try to comply as far as reasonably practicable.

8.5 Summary

In summary, it is important not to overlook the issues raised in this chapter. Termination provisions may represent a simpler way of resolving any potential dispute but need to be complied with carefully. The Government's guidance note, together with good faith considerations, also serve as a reminder that parties should look to resolve their differences as amicably as possible.

8.6 Practical steps

- locate termination clauses and check their contents carefully
- if appropriate, consider terminating the contract
- locate good faith clauses and review whether they will be interpreted narrowly or broadly
- consider whether the contract falls within the definition of 'relational contract' set out in Yam Seng
- consider the effect of the implied terms tests
- review the government's guidance note and be prepared to demonstrate how you complied with it
- if another party acts in breach of the principles set out in the guidance note make a note of this and use it as evidence of bad faith

CHAPTER NINE
COMMERCIAL ALTERNATIVES

9.1 Introduction

The first reaction of many contracting parties in the light of Covid-19 is to reach for the force majeure clause and then think about frustration. However, although there is nothing wrong with this approach, it is also worthwhile considering what commercial alternatives may have been available.

9.2 Disaster Recovery Plans

One issue that is regularly raised when negotiating larger contracts, is the extent to which a service provider is required to put in place back up plans that could ensure continuity of service in the event of a force majeure event.

An example of this might be a car insurance broker which provides white labelled insurance products for leading brands. These products would typically be provided both via the internet and also via call centres. In some cases the service provider may be required to maintain a reserve call centre that could be made operational in 24 hours assuming one of its existing call centres was no longer operable. Alongside this there may well be a requirement to have reserve servers and extra back ups of data in the event that its main servers were damaged in some way. The benefit of having such clauses is obvious in that they ensure continuity of service and avoid arguments about force majeure or frustration.

In the context of Covid-19, perhaps the most relevant consideration would be whether the disaster recovery plans allowed employees to continue to work securely from home so that they could continue to provide the services even though they cannot physically attend work.

If such plans are not included at present, then it may be a good opportunity to insert them now with a view to further waves of Covid-19 or indeed the effect of other similar future events.

9.3 Business interruption cover

There has been considerable discussion about this issue as a result of Covid-19. Some businesses will not have this cover and therefore should seriously think about obtaining such cover in future. Other businesses will have this cover but are currently encountering resistance from insurers seeking to avoid payouts. This is likely to lead to considerable litigation in the future.

9.4 Re-negotiation

If there are no specific disaster recovery plans nor business interruption cover then the most appropriate course of action is to consider some form of re-negotiation in respect of the terms of the contract. This idea was mentioned in respect of mitigation in chapter 4 but I will now set out a little more detail about how this process could work in practice.

9.4.1 Key areas for re-negotiation

These are as follows:

(i) Re-arrangement of dates

In some cases, the re-arrangement of dates may be feasible for both parties and this should be tried wherever possible as a first step.

(ii) Extension of contract period

If re-arrangement of dates is not possible the next thing to consider is an extension of the contract period so that the parties have more flexibility about the time it takes to perform their obligations.

(iii) Amendment of key obligations

Another possibility is to mutually agree that one or both of the parties will be released from some or all of their obligations for a specified time period with a corresponding reduction in fees where appropriate.

(iv) Reduction in fees

Where one of the parties wishes to be released from its obligations to pay, due to financial difficulties arising from Covid-19, then this could be agreed in exchange for:

- a corresponding uplift once the fall-out from Covid-19 has come to an end
- a longer contract period
- removal of a break clause so as to ensure that the contract cannot be terminated in this way during the remainder of its duration

9.4.2 Variation of obligations

Of course, all of these proposed changes would need to be documented carefully. In particular, the parties would need to pay careful attention to any variation clause contained within the contract as this may contain specific requirements in respect of format and content of the variation.

A typical variation clause would read as follows:

> *'Any variation of this Agreement shall not be effective unless made in writing and signed by or on behalf of each of the Parties to this Agreement.'*

The key points to note in respect of such a clause are as follows:

- this clause would permit a valid variation via exchange of e-mails[1]
- this clause would not permit an oral variation that was not reduced to writing[2]

It should also be remembered that a valid variation requires consideration and therefore, although a variation letter can suffice, parties may often choose to execute a deed of variation to avoid any arguments.

9.5 Summary

In summary, there are a number of ways whereby the parties can agree to 'share the pain' so that the contract endures and both parties ultimately will be able to survive. This more gracious approach to resolving Covid-19 disputes also reflects the Government's comments in its guidance note referred to in the previous chapter.

9.6 Practical steps

- consider whether the existing contract contains disaster recovery provisions

---

1 C&S Associates v Enterprise [2015] EWHC 3757 (Comm)

2 MWB Business Exchange Centres Ltd v Rock Advertising Ltd [2018] UKSC 24

- if not, consider whether they need to be added in respect of future events
- consider the availability of business interruption insurance
- if you do not have this at present, consider whether it should be added to your business insurance policy in the future
- consider whether re-negotiation is possible
- ensure that any contract variations are carefully recorded and that the requirements of the variation clause are complied with

PART C

APPENDICES

1. Coronavirus Act 2020 Overview
2. The Health Protection (Coronavirus, Restrictions) (England) Regulations 2020
3. Timeline
4. Resources

APPENDIX ONE
CORONAVIRUS ACT 2020
OVERVIEW

PART 1 Main provisions

Interpretation

1. Meaning of "coronavirus" and related terminology

Emergency registration of health professionals

2. Emergency registration of nurses and other health and care professionals
3. Emergency arrangements concerning medical practitioners: Wales
4. Emergency arrangements concerning medical practitioners: Scotland
5. Emergency registration of and extension of prescribing powers for pharmaceutical chemists: Northern Ireland

Temporary registration of social workers

6. Emergency registration of social workers: England and Wales
7. Temporary registration of social workers: Scotland

Emergency volunteers

8. Emergency volunteering leave
9. Compensation for emergency volunteers

Mental health and mental capacity

10. Temporary modification of mental health and mental capacity legislation

Health service indemnification

11. Indemnity for health service activity: England and Wales
12. Indemnity for health service activity: Scotland
13. Indemnity for health and social care activity: Northern Ireland

NHS and local authority care and support

14. NHS Continuing Healthcare assessments: England
15. Local authority care and support
16. Duty of local authority to assess needs: Scotland
17. Section 16: further provision

Registration of deaths and still-births etc

18. Registration of deaths and still-births etc
19. Confirmatory medical certificate not required for cremations: England and Wales
20. Review of cause of death certificates and cremations: Scotland
21. Modifications of requirements regarding medical certificates for cremations: Northern Ireland

Investigatory powers

22. Appointment of temporary Judicial Commissioners
23. Time limits in relation to urgent warrants etc under Investigatory Powers Act

Fingerprints and DNA profiles

24. Extension of time limits for retention of fingerprints and DNA profiles

Food supply

25. Power to require information relating to food supply chains
26. Authorities which may require information
27. Restrictions on use and disclosure of information
28. Enforcement of requirement to provide information
29. Meaning of "food supply chain" and related expressions

Inquests

30. Suspension of requirement to hold inquest with jury: England and Wales
31. Suspension of requirement to hold inquest with jury: Northern Ireland
32. Deaths in custody from natural illness: Northern Ireland

Disclosure: Wales

33. Disapplication etc by Welsh Ministers of DBS provisions

Disclosure: Scotland

34. Temporary disapplication of disclosure offences: Scotland
35. Power to reclassify certain disclosure requests: Scotland

Vaccinations: Scotland

36. Vaccination and immunisation: Scotland

Schools, childcare providers etc

37. Temporary closure of educational institutions and childcare premises
38. Temporary continuity: education, training and childcare

Statutory sick pay

39. Statutory sick pay: funding of employers' liabilities
40. Statutory sick pay: power to disapply waiting period limitation
41. Statutory sick pay: modification of regulation making powers
42. Statutory sick pay: funding of employers' liabilities: Northern Ireland
43. Statutory sick pay: power to disapply waiting period limitation: Northern Ireland
44. Statutory sick pay: modification of regulation making powers: Northern Ireland

Pensions

45. NHS pension schemes: suspension of restrictions on return to work: England and Wales
46. NHS pension schemes: suspension of restrictions on return to work: Scotland
47. Health and social care pension schemes: suspension of restrictions on return to work: Northern Ireland

Protection of public health

48. Powers to act for the protection of public health: Northern Ireland
49. Health protection regulations: Scotland

Power to suspend port operations

50. Power to suspend port operations

Powers relating to potentially infectious persons

51. Powers relating to potentially infectious persons

Powers relating to events, gatherings and premises

52. Powers to issue directions relating to events, gatherings and premises

Courts and tribunals: use of video and audio technology

53. Expansion of availability of live links in criminal proceedings
54. Expansion of availability of live links in other criminal hearings
55. Public participation in proceedings conducted by video or audio
56. Live links in magistrates' court appeals against requirements or restrictions imposed on a potentially infectious person
57. Use of live links in legal proceedings: Northern Ireland

Powers in relation to bodies

58. Powers in relation to transportation, storage and disposal of dead bodies etc

Postponement of elections, referendums, recall petitions and canvass

59. Elections and referendums due to be held in England in period after 15 March 2020
60. Postponement of elections due to be held on 7 May 2020
61. Power to postpone certain other elections and referendums
62. Power to postpone a recall petition under the Recall of MPs Act 2015
63. Power to make supplementary etc provision
64. Northern Ireland: timing of canvass and Assembly by-elections

Postponement of elections: Wales

65. Elections due to be held in Wales in period after 15 March 2020
66. Postponement of National Assembly for Wales elections for constituency vacancies

67. Power to postpone local authority elections in Wales for casual vacancies
68. Power to make supplementary etc provision

Postponement of elections: Scotland

69. Postponement of Scottish Parliament elections for constituency vacancies
70. Postponement of local authority elections in Scotland for casual vacancies

Other administrative requirements

71. Signatures of Treasury Commissioners

National Insurance Contributions

72. Power under section 143 of the Social Security Administration Act 1992
73. Power under section 145 of the Social Security Administration Act 1992
74. Power under section 5 of the National Insurance Contributions Act 2014

Financial assistance for industry

75. Disapplication of limit under section 8 of the Industrial Development Act 1982

HMRC functions

76. HMRC functions

89. Expiry
90. Power to alter expiry date
91. Power to amend Act in consequence of amendments to subordinate legislation
92. Power to make consequential modifications
93. Procedure for certain regulations made by a Minister of the Crown
94. Procedure for certain regulations made by the Welsh Ministers
95. Procedure for certain regulations made by the Scottish Ministers
96. Procedure for certain orders made by a Northern Ireland department
97. Reports by Secretary of State on status of non-devolved provisions of this Act
98. Six-month parliamentary review
99. Parliamentary consideration of status of non-devolved provisions of this Act
100. Extent
101. Extension to the Isle of Man
102. Short title

SCHEDULES

SCHEDULE 1 Emergency registration of nurses and other health and care professionals

SCHEDULE 2 Emergency arrangements concerning medical practitioners: Wales

SCHEDULE 3 Emergency arrangements concerning medical practitioners: Scotland

SCHEDULE 4 Emergency registration of pharmaceutical chemists and extension of prescribing powers: Northern Ireland

SCHEDULE 5 Emergency registration of social workers: England and Wales

SCHEDULE 6 Temporary registration of social workers: Scotland

SCHEDULE 7 Emergency volunteering leave

SCHEDULE 8 Mental health: England and Wales

SCHEDULE 9 Mental health: Scotland

SCHEDULE 10 Mental health: Northern Ireland

SCHEDULE 11 Mental capacity: Northern Ireland

SCHEDULE 12 Local authority care and support

SCHEDULE 13 Registration of deaths and still-births

SCHEDULE 14 Review of medical certificates of cause of death and cremations: Scotland

SCHEDULE 15 Information relating to food supply chains: financial penalties

SCHEDULE 16 Temporary closure of educational institutions and childcare premises

SCHEDULE 17 Temporary continuity directions etc: education, training and childcare

SCHEDULE 18 Powers to act for the protection of public health: Northern Ireland

SCHEDULE 19 Health protection regulations: Scotland

SCHEDULE 20 Power to suspend port operations

SCHEDULE 21 Powers relating to potentially infectious persons

SCHEDULE 22 Powers to issue directions relating to events, gatherings and premises

SCHEDULE 23 Live links in criminal proceedings

SCHEDULE 24 Live links in other criminal hearings

SCHEDULE 25 Public participation in proceedings conducted by video or audio

SCHEDULE 26 Live links in certain magistrates' court proceedings

SCHEDULE 27 Use of live links in legal proceedings: Northern Ireland

SCHEDULE 28 Transportation, storage and disposal of dead bodies etc

SCHEDULE 29 Residential tenancies in England and Wales: protection from eviction

APPENDIX TWO
THE HEALTH PROTECTION (CORONAVIRUS, RESTRICTIONS) (ENGLAND) REGULATIONS 2020

1. Citation, commencement, application and interpretation
2. Revocation and saving
3. The emergency period and review of need for restrictions
4. Requirement to close premises and businesses during the emergency
5. Further restrictions and closures during the emergency period
6. Restrictions on movement
7. Restrictions on gatherings
8. Enforcement of requirement
9. Offences and penalties
10. Fixed penalty notices
11. Prosecutions
12. Expiry

SCHEDULE 1 — Underlying Medical Conditions

1. Chronic (long-term) respiratory diseases, such as asthma, chronic obstructive pulmonary...
2. Chronic heart disease, such as heart failure.
3. Chronic kidney disease.
4. Chronic liver disease, such as hepatitis.
5. Chronic neurological conditions, such as Parkinson's disease, motor neurone disease...
6. Diabetes.
7. Problems with the spleen, such as sickle cell disease or...
8. A weakened immune system as the result of conditions such...
9. Being seriously overweight, with a body mass index of 40...

SCHEDULE 2 — Businesses subject to restrictions or closure

PART 1

1. Restaurants, including restaurants and dining rooms in hotels or members'
2. (1) Cafes, including workplace canteens (subject to sub-paragraph (2)),
3. Bars, including bars in hotels or members' clubs.
4. Public houses.

PART 2

5. Cinemas.
6. Theatres.
7. Nightclubs.
8. Bingo halls.
9. Concert halls.
10. Museums and galleries.
11. Casinos.
12. Betting shops.
13. Spas.
14. Nail, beauty, hair salons and barbers.
15. Massage parlours.
16. Tattoo and piercing parlours.
17. Skating rinks.
18. Indoor fitness studios, gyms, swimming pools, bowling alleys, amusement arcades...
19. Funfairs (whether outdoors or indoors).
20. Playgrounds, indoor sports courts, outdoor gyms and outdoor swimming...
21. Outdoor markets (except for livestock markets and stalls selling food)...
22. Car showrooms.
23. Auction Houses (except for livestock auctions).

PART 3

24. Food retailers, including food markets, supermarkets, convenience stores and corner...
25. Off licenses and licensed shops selling alcohol (including breweries).
26. Pharmacies (including non-dispensing pharmacies) and chemists.
27. Newsagents.
28. Homeware, building supplies and hardware stores.
29. Petrol stations.
30. Car repair and MOT services.
31. Bicycle shops.
32. Taxi or vehicle hire businesses.
33. The following businesses—
(a) banks,
(b) building societies,
(c) credit unions,
(d) short term loan providers,
(e) savings clubs,
(f) cash points, and
(g) undertakings which by way of business operate currency exchange offices, transmit money (or any representation of money) by any means or cash cheques which are made payable to customers.
34. Post offices.
35. Funeral directors.
36. Laundrettes and dry cleaners.
37. Dental services, opticians, audiology services, chiropody, chiropractors, osteopaths and other...
38. Veterinary surgeons and pet shops.
39. Agricultural supplies shop.
40. Storage and distribution facilities, including delivery drop off or collection...
41. Car parks.
42. Public toilets.
43. Garden centres.
44. Outdoor sports courts.

APPENDIX THREE
TIMELINE

Date	Event
11th March 2020	Covid-19 declared a pandemic by the WHO
21st March 2020	Health Protection (Coronavirus, Business Closure) (England) Regulations 2020 (NB revoked on 26th March 2020)
25th March 2020	Coronavirus Act 2020
26th March 2020	The Health Protection (Coronavirus, Restrictions) (England) Regulations 2020
22nd April 2020	The Health Protection (Coronavirus, Restrictions) (England) (Amendment) Regulations 2020
13th May 2020	The Health Protection (Coronavirus, Restrictions) (England) (Amendment) (No. 2) Regulations 2020
1st June 2020	The Health Protection (Coronavirus, Restrictions) (England) (Amendment) (No. 3) Regulations 2020

APPENDIX FOUR
RESOURCES

4.1 Legislation

Coronavirus Act 2020

http://www.legislation.gov.uk/ukpga/2020/7/contents

The Health Protection (Coronavirus, Restrictions) (England) Regulations 2020

http://www.legislation.gov.uk/uksi/2020/350/contents

The Health Protection (Coronavirus, Restrictions) (England) (Amendment) Regulations 2020

http://www.legislation.gov.uk/uksi/2020/447/contents/made

The Health Protection (Coronavirus, Restrictions) (England) (Amendment) (No. 2) Regulations 2020

http://www.legislation.gov.uk/uksi/2020/500/contents/made

The Health Protection (Coronavirus, Restrictions) (England) (Amendment) (No. 3) Regulations 2020

http://www.legislation.gov.uk/uksi/2020/558/pdfs/uksi_20200558_en.pdf

4.2 Guidance

CMA Guidance

Covid-19 – pandemic, consumer contracts, cancellation and refunds – 30th April 2020

https://www.gov.uk/government/publications/cma-to-investigate-concerns-about-cancellation-policies-during-the-coronavirus-covid-19-pandemic/the-coronavirus-covid-19-pandemic-consumer-contracts-cancellation-and-refunds

Contract Guidance

Guidance on responsible contractual behaviour in the performance and enforcement of contracts impacted by the Covid-19 emergency

https://www.gov.uk/government/publications/guidance-on-responsible-contractual-behaviour-in-the-performance-and-enforcement-of-contracts-impacted-by-the-covid-19-emergency

MORE BOOKS BY LAW BRIEF PUBLISHING

A selection of our other titles available now:-

'A Practical Guide to the General Data Protection Regulation (GDPR) – 2nd Edition' by Keith Markham
'Ellis on Credit Hire – Sixth Edition' by Aidan Ellis & Tim Kevan
'A Practical Guide to Working with Litigants in Person and McKenzie Friends in Family Cases' by Stuart Barlow
'Protecting Unregistered Brands: A Practical Guide to the Law of Passing Off' by Lorna Brazell
'A Practical Guide to Secondary Liability and Joint Enterprise Post-Jogee' by Joanne Cecil & James Mehigan
'A Practical Guide to the Pre-Action RTA Claims Protocol for Personal Injury Lawyers' by Antonia Ford
'A Practical Guide to Neighbour Disputes and the Law' by Alexander Walsh
'A Practical Guide to Forfeiture of Leases' by Mark Shelton
'A Practical Guide to Coercive Control for Legal Practitioners and Victims' by Rachel Horman
'A Practical Guide to Rights Over Airspace and Subsoil' by Daniel Gatty
'Tackling Disclosure in the Criminal Courts – A Practitioner's Guide' by Narita Bahra QC & Don Ramble
'A Practical Guide to the Law of Driverless Cars – Second Edition' by Alex Glassbrook, Emma Northey & Scarlett Milligan
'A Practical Guide to TOLATA Claims' by Greg Williams
'Artificial Intelligence – The Practical Legal Issues' by John Buyers
'A Practical Guide to the Law of Prescription in Scotland' by Andrew Foyle
'A Practical Guide to the Construction and Rectification of Wills and Trust Instruments' by Edward Hewitt
'A Practical Guide to the Law of Bullying and Harassment in the Workplace' by Philip Hyland

'How to Be a Freelance Solicitor: A Practical Guide to the SRA-Regulated Freelance Solicitor Model' by Paul Bennett
'A Practical Guide to Prison Injury Claims' by Malcolm Johnson
'A Practical Guide to the Small Claims Track' by Dominic Bright
'A Practical Guide to Advising Clients at the Police Station' by Colin Stephen McKeown-Beaumont
'A Practical Guide to Antisocial Behaviour Injunctions' by Iain Wightwick
'Practical Mediation: A Guide for Mediators, Advocates, Advisers, Lawyers, and Students in Civil, Commercial, Business, Property, Workplace, and Employment Cases' by Jonathan Dingle with John Sephton
'The Mini-Pupillage Workbook' by David Boyle
'A Practical Guide to Crofting Law' by Brian Inkster
'A Practical Guide to Spousal Maintenance' by Liz Cowell
'A Practical Guide to the Law of Domain Names and Cybersquatting' by Andrew Clemson
'A Practical Guide to the Law of Gender Pay Gap Reporting' by Harini Iyengar
'A Practical Guide to the Rights of Grandparents in Children Proceedings' by Stuart Barlow
'NHS Whistleblowing and the Law' by Joseph England
'Employment Law and the Gig Economy' by Nigel Mackay & Annie Powell
'A Practical Guide to Noise Induced Hearing Loss (NIHL) Claims' by Andrew Mckie, Ian Skeate, Gareth McAloon
'An Introduction to Beauty Negligence Claims – A Practical Guide for the Personal Injury Practitioner' by Greg Almond
'Intercompany Agreements for Transfer Pricing Compliance' by Paul Sutton
'Zen and the Art of Mediation' by Martin Plowman
'A Practical Guide to the SRA Principles, Individual and Law Firm Codes of Conduct 2019 – What Every Law Firm Needs to Know' by Paul Bennett
'A Practical Guide to Adoption for Family Lawyers' by Graham Pegg
'A Practical Guide to Industrial Disease Claims' by Andrew Mckie & Ian Skeate
'A Practical Guide to Redundancy' by Philip Hyland
'A Practical Guide to Vicarious Liability' by Mariel Irvine

‘A Practical Guide to Applications for Landlord’s Consent and Variation of Leases’ by Mark Shelton
‘A Practical Guide to Relief from Sanctions Post-Mitchell and Denton’ by Peter Causton
‘A Practical Guide to Equity Release for Advisors’ by Paul Sams
‘A Practical Guide to Unlawful Eviction and Harassment’ by Stephanie Lovegrove
‘A Practical Guide to the Law Relating to Food’ by Ian Thomas
‘A Practical Guide to Financial Services Claims’ by Chris Hegarty
‘The Law of Houses in Multiple Occupation: A Practical Guide to HMO Proceedings’ by Julian Hunt
‘A Practical Guide to Unlawful Eviction and Harassment’ by Stephanie Lovegrove
‘A Practical Guide to Solicitor and Client Costs’ by Robin Dunne
‘Occupiers, Highways and Defective Premises Claims: A Practical Guide Post-Jackson – 2nd Edition’ by Andrew Mckie
‘A Practical Guide to Financial Ombudsman Service Claims’ by Adam Temple & Robert Scrivenor
‘A Practical Guide to the Law of Enfranchisement and Lease Extension’ by Paul Sams
‘A Practical Guide to Marketing for Lawyers – 2nd Edition’ by Catherine Bailey & Jennet Ingram
'A Practical Guide to Advising Schools on Employment Law' by Jonathan Holden
‘A Practical Guide to Running Housing Disrepair and Cavity Wall Claims: 2nd Edition’ by Andrew Mckie & Ian Skeate
‘A Practical Guide to Holiday Sickness Claims – 2nd Edition’ by Andrew Mckie & Ian Skeate
‘Arguments and Tactics for Personal Injury and Clinical Negligence Claims’ by Dorian Williams
‘A Practical Guide to QOCS and Fundamental Dishonesty’ by James Bentley
‘A Practical Guide to Drone Law’ by Rufus Ballaster, Andrew Firman, Eleanor Clot
‘A Practical Guide to Compliance for Personal Injury Firms Working With Claims Management Companies’ by Paul Bennett
‘A Practical Guide to the Landlord and Tenant Act 1954: Commercial Tenancies’ by Richard Hayes & David Sawtell

www.ingramcontent.com/pod-product-compliance
Lightning Source LLC
LaVergne TN
LVHW022052200926
848481LV00003B/882
* 9 7 8 1 9 1 3 7 1 5 0 5 2 *